JOHN BERGER AND ME

Also by Nikos Papastergiadis

Modernity as Exile: The Stranger in John Berger's Writing
Dialogues in the Diasporas: Essays and Conversations on Cultural Identity
The Turbulence of Migration
Metaphor and Tension: On Collaboration and its Discontents
Spatial Aesthetics: Essays on Art, Place and the Everyday
Cosmopolitanism and Culture
Ambient Perspectives
Museums of the Commons: L'International and the Crisis of Europe
On Art and Friendship
The Cosmos in Cosmopolitanism

NIKOS PAPASTERGIADIS

JOHN BERGER AND ME: A MIGRANT'S EYE

Published 2024
from the Writing and Society Research Centre
at Western Sydney University
by the Giramondo Publishing Company
PO Box 752
Artarmon NSW 1570 Australia
www.giramondopublishing.com

Designed by Jenny Grigg
Typeset by Andrew Davies
in Tiempos Regular 9/15pt

Cover image: Sarah Curtis

Printed and bound by Pegasus Media & Logistics
Distributed in Australia by NewSouth Books

A catalogue record for this book is available from the National Library of Australia.

ISBN 978-1-923106-12-3

9 8 7 6 5 4 3 2 1

The Giramondo Publishing Company acknowledges the support of Western Sydney University in the implementation of its book publishing program.

This project has been assisted by the Commonwealth Government through Creative Australia, its arts funding and advisory body.

For Yves

Contents

1. Stories from the Kitchen

John Berger will be 100 in 2026. He was born in South London and died at the age of ninety in the suburbs of Paris. This is a book about how he changed my appreciation of my father's peasant life and how his memory continues to shape my life. In a helix-like manner it follows John's journey from the metropolis to the village and my father's migration, the peasant who becomes a factory worker in Melbourne.

John's father, Stanley, fought in the First World War, gained the Military Cross, and lost his faith. At the end of his career, Stanley was also decorated for his contribution to public accounting. His mother, Miriam, was a working-class woman and a suffragette. She enjoyed taking John to the cinema. They sent him to boarding school at the age of six. After his military service John attended art school. At the age of thirty he discovered that his real talent was writing on art and politics. Soon after he found another gift, the capacity to speak before a camera. He addressed the camera as if it were a means for delivering an urgent message to a friend in need.

In the second half of his life, he and his partner Anya Bostock, along with their two children Katya and Jacob, left England. Anya was a writer and translator. She exposed him to feminism and continental philosophy. They lived first in France and then in 1962 they settled in Geneva. John always felt uncomfortable with the Swiss.

During the promotion of his books at the 1973 Frankfurt Book Fair, he met Beverly Bancroft who was the rights manager of Penguin in the UK. John left Anya and Geneva. John and Beverly moved to the Haute-Savoie in France and had a son called Yves.

Nella Bielski was born in the Ukraine. She was an actor and writer who emigrated to France after she married a journalist. She met John in Paris in the early 1980s. They fell in love and collaborated to write the play *A Question of Geography*.

Despite the initial conflict of sharing his life with two women, John split his time between the city and the country. Part of the year he was with Nella in the suburb of St Antony. However, in the haymaking season he was always in Quincy in the Haute-Savoie.

John wrote about many of the big themes of his time. As a critic he was drawn to art that exposed injustice and expanded consciousness. He wrote film scripts about sexual liberation, told stories about the disappearing peasantry, and the protagonists in his later novels were usually urban fringe-dwellers. He claimed that the book that was most revealing of him was *A Seventh Man*. It is a portrait of the *Gastarbeiter*. It is written from the migrant's eye. When my mother read the Greek translation, she sighed. 'This is my story. It is written as if he were sitting on my shoulders.'

A recurring beat in all of John's work is the loss and love of home.

This is also a book about the attraction to art and knowledge. The loss of faith in politics and the awkward process of becoming my own man.

I come from peasants and their love of teachers. My father's family were from the mountains in northern Greece. The village Skalohori was named after a ladder – *skala*. They moved it up and down the mountain for safety. For hundreds of generations, they lived a simple life of subsistence, nothing much changed until the Germans arrived in the Second World War. The Nazis burnt their houses and shot my grandfather. He was just walking home. The village was torched twice again by the Greek government army during the Civil War. Many in the village were communists. One of my uncles had a sparkling intelligence and a brilliant voice. He caught the attention of the fur traders in the nearby town of Kastoria. They sponsored him to go to Paris, where he studied and was influenced by Piaget's theory of child education. He returned and became a dean at the polytechnic in Thessaloniki. My father's village was then nicknamed 'teacher-village' or Daskalohori, which in Greek rhymes with ladder-village. The dean baptised many children and was the *meson* – the medium – for the boys in the village. Many got degrees. My father worked in the kitchen of the polytechnic.

My mother Eleni was the firstborn with three younger brothers. She loved school and her father adored her. She would burn too much oil in the lantern, and he giggled that he would make her a teacher. He was shot during the Civil War while dancing at a baptism in a neighbouring village. My mother and her three brothers were sent to an orphanage. She sent tear-soaked letters begging to come home and help with kitchen duties. For three months she wore a smock twice her size and sat under a tree without a teacher. My grandmother eventually gathered the resources to bring her and her brother Nikiforos home, and then when my mother was old enough to care for the twins they went back for Yiorgos and Telemachus. When she returned to the village she cried until she was allowed to join her classmates in third year of primary school.

John Berger died on 2 January 2017. In 1972 he won the Booker Prize for his novel *G* and made the TV series and book *Ways of Seeing*. This was a book that played a vital role in transforming the art world. In that decade public education in the UK and Australia produced a previously unthinkable outcome. Working-class kids, like Damien Hirst in Leeds, started to dream of becoming artists. In the following decade the arrival of the Sex Pistols not only redefined the production of music but crashed down barriers in art schools.

The art world was still dominated by cravat-wearing connoisseurs, aristocratic collectors and haughty curators. There was no sign at the entrance of museums that said: 'migrants and the working classes are not welcome', but I wonder how many mothers said to their sons, 'art is for the rich'.

Dean is the son of Croatian migrants. He drives forklifts. He has almond-shaped eyes and cheekbones that outshine Marcello Mastroianni. He was sitting next to me at our daughters' graduation dinner. He looked up at the stained-glass ceiling designed by Leonard French in the great hall of the National Gallery of Victoria. His mouth stayed open. His eyes remained transfixed.

'You know, when I am in Europe, I visit the museums in every city. But here in Melbourne, I have never been in this building before.'

John's words in *Ways of Seeing* were both plaintive and polemical. What he said was in the spirit of welcome, but his luxurious tone and lisp was still part of the world we wanted to overthrow. His voice was not out of place on the BBC. I read *Ways of Seeing* in 1980. The book was a provocation against formalist art history. It took aim at the snobs and gave voice to the thought that art and politics could enrich each other. As with so many undergraduates, the book became my companion. It arrived in my world as if it had already been part of my life, and it served as a lexicon for making sense of the things to come. I experienced this spirit of articulation and extension in all his subsequent books that I read. After he died, I expected that new books would continue to appear on the shelves of bookshops. Of course, this is impossible. Death is a full stop. He did not have an infinite realm of manuscripts hidden in a box under the bed. However, the finality of his death was also a reordering of the inner architecture of my relationship with him and his books. His absence after his death was nothing like the absence I experienced before I knew of his existence. After the loss of a companion there is grief. Before the knowledge of such a person there is a different kind of solitude. In between there is a change in the horizon of possibilities. John came into my life like a companion.

I still find myself talking about John, ruminating with him in my mind, and every time I tell a story to a friend, it is as if John is at the other end of the kitchen table. When I notice a big elm tree, feel angry at the injustices in the world, or enjoy the company of strangers, I feel as if John's belly is pressing against the side of my arms and his cologne is wafting between us. If Sartre's maxim is true, that people's stay in heaven is dependent on the extent that other people keep talking about them on earth, then John, I am sure you are hearing all of this. It feels like yesterday that you were reading the text you wrote for Juan Munoz.

Who does not know what it is like to go with a friend to a railway station
and then to watch the train take them away? As you walk along the
platform back into the city, the person who has just gone is often more
there, more totally there, than when you embraced them before they
climbed into the train. When we embrace to say good-bye, maybe we
do it for this reason – to take into our arms what we want to keep when
they've gone.[1]

When John moved to a peasant village, Quincy in the French Alps, he began a trilogy called *Into Their Labours*. The first volume, *Pig Earth*, was a collection of stories on the survival of the peasants. In the second volume, *Once in Europa*, there is the tracing of their journeys to the city. And the final part of the trilogy, *Lilac and Flag*, is a novel that tells the story of the children of migrants as they live on the edges of the city and the law. The stories of struggle and loss in *Pig Earth* find a summit in 'The Three Lives of Lucie Cabrol'. Lucie was born without advantage. She was tiny at birth, but she forever compensated with a ferocity for scavenging and the ingenuity of a smuggler. Only in her third life, when she is already dead, is she desired. The man who rejected her twice before, sees her as if for the first time, from the other side of the frontier. He sees her beauty and also sees how he has wasted his life elsewhere, as a migrant in Paris, Buenos Aires and Montreal. Finally, Lucie reveals to him that the surplus in the barn of the dead never ends.

The tales of the departed pervade the short stories in *Once in Europa*. I recognise the feeling of loss that John portrayed in his characters. The fragility of a life that was attached to the land is deepened with sadness of loves that remained unrequited. 'As the night drew on and the cows in the stable lay down on their bedding of straw and beech leaves, the warmth of his body penetrated her absence so that it became his own pain.'

'The absence of the mourned is as precise as their presence once was.' (*Once in Europa*, 15)

The dead are with us.

My mother took me to a concert by Manos Hadjidakis. He was alone with a piano on stage at the Melbourne Town Hall. I was only fifteen and I knew very little about music. But looking down at his hands from the balcony was a mesmerising experience. I cannot recall the duration, was it tiny or infinite? One thing is for sure, I leant forward and did not move. Thirty years later I met the legendary singer Savina Yannatou in Rhodes. Her band was performing for a conference at which I was giving a keynote speech. I was enthralled to be so close to her voice which, during a dozen songs, stretched across the whole of the Mediterranean. We joined her for dinner after the concert. She was pleased that I wrote about art and seeing the opportunity to connect me with a friend who was a painter in Athens, she arranged a rendezvous at a tavern. We sat under a vine that grew in the shadow of the Hilton hotel. Savina pointed out the bar which Manos frequented.

Like a sleepwalker I went in.

A few steps down there was a long-cushioned bench. I saw Manos reclining there. With his eyes closed, his belly and smile were fully enjoying the late afternoon siesta.

Manos had died five years earlier. But his presence was as real there in the bar at Pangrati as it was at the concert in Melbourne.

I squirm with the thought of the number of times you said this to me: 'Write stories like the way you tell them when we are all gathered here in the kitchen!' You were never anti-intellectual, but you had no time for what you called the 'constipated style' of academics.

It is true. When I was writing about migrant experiences, referring to artistic practices and interpreting philosophical concepts I pressed too many things together. There was almost no breathing space. I also suffered from a typical academic anxiety. As an Indian mentor put it, 'You are trying to master everything at once for fear of not looking dumb.'

You ran away from school. I was more obedient.

I was jealous of people who could ruthlessly pursue their art. However, I was conflicted: on the one hand I was repulsed by the sight of others who held everyone hostage to their own ego, and on the other I struggled to preserve my independence. I thought it was ugly to bully others into the service of my art and so I was determined to pay my own way. My father always said you only buy when you have 'cash money'. You can promise only what you have already saved in your barn. How would writing pay my rent? Two women offered a life where they would cover the cost of our living. That made me feel like a failure. It made me flee. I could not shake off my father's ideal of being the provider. When I eventually became a father, I did not have the self-belief to elevate my artistic creation over my family. In fact, I would steal time to write and hide any success that came my way.

In 1962 you emigrated from England to Geneva. In the same year I was born in Australia. At the point in life when most successful authors look for comfort you found another life in a peasant village. You arrived in a place akin to the place which my parents had left. You were a prominent art critic and celebrated author. I dreamed of the life you had lived. When I told my mother that I wanted to be a writer she sighed: 'That is a luxury that only the rich can indulge. Maybe your children will be artists.'

I took your stories as portals into a past of mine that had no archive. Remember that first phone call – I told you about my Uncle Yiorgo who ran away from the village, joined the circus and toured the Balkans performing 'the wheel of death' on a motorcycle.

For two years we were all stuck at home. At first, I wrote without access to my library. The Covid blues meant no travel, but a flood of memories. This book came from this forced freedom. I both believe in my memories and accept that some have been warped with time. My overall aim is not to recreate an historical record but to offer what you call a 'likeness'. It is a portrait based on a sequence of anecdotes, which I present now as fragments that give a glimpse of your wisdom and hospitality.

It is also a process of self-discovery. You have been where I was heading towards. My parents left the kind of village that you arrived at. The parallels and intersections prompted me to ask what sort of a man I wanted to be. Could art serve as a bridge between these worlds?

In the midst of Cold War debates on art and politics you took a strident position. In the collection of essays that you had written in the 1950s for the *New Statesman* you asserted that: 'imagination is not, as it is sometimes thought, the ability to invent; it is the capacity to disclose that which exists'. (*Permanent Red*, 51) At this point in time, you stressed that the revelatory function of the imagination was to be given a determinant role over all other dimensions. You insisted that the duty of the artist was defined in terms of a pursuit of truth.

Repeatedly, you returned to the point that art was imbued with a strong corrective task: it was meant to clarify ambiguities, break out of restrictions and overcome false hierarchies. Through art we could *see through* the distortions that blurred reality, blocked solidarity and delayed justice. You were accused of becoming a foghorn. You replied: 'What could be more useful in this English weather.'

However, that is not the full picture. Whoever only saw the fighter in you missed the point. For you, art is not just a representation of reality. Its function is not confined to either revelation or decoration. It is essential to life. Art is not apart from or even opposed to reality, it is a way in which reality is constituted. It comes from the interchange of signals sent and received. To exist is to create. And yet art has no real purpose, let alone any certainty. It would be a meagre life, but it is not impossible to be without it. For art is not tied to need but only to the wondrous questions and answers we give in search of meaning. This is a surplus, but without it there is no civilisation.

Twenty years ago, I discussed my plan with you to work with Merryn Gates on an exhibition and symposium on your influence in Australian art. Merryn called it *What Berger Saw*, and the exhibition eventually toured the country. I edited a small book drawn from the symposium. While I was talking about it, you started to fidget with your sleeves, rolling them up, unrolling them. You ran your fingers through your hair, and then jumped up to go to the sink and wash the dishes.

You were always an enthusiastic cook, but washing up, this was a job for Yves.

You came back to the table to dry the Opinel knives. This made sense because they rust if they are left damp. But then you grumbled: 'Isn't there something else more important to do in Australia?'[2]

I laughed. It could be taken as a colonial put down.

I was sure that your comment came from your abhorrence at the idea of being put up on a pedestal. You had no interest in guarding your legacy as if it were a unique fortress, or even worse, of being set up as a standard against which others were measured.

To clear the air, I explained the ways in which people have picked ideas from your books and stretched them into different directions. The project, I stressed, was not an homage but an exploration of shared aims. Suddenly, you relaxed.

I, like many others, have felt that your stories have given words to our private but only half-worked-out hopes. When we read you, it is as if you are speaking *from* us. Then there is the feeling that we are walking all together. Your voice stays in our head long after we have put down your books. It is there in a conversational and authoritative manner, combining plaintive and agitated tones, proceeding towards an open but pointed objective. The places that you evoke seem to come from the other side of our windows. The people in your stories seem to be walking amongst us. You ended a letter to me once with an apology: 'In haste to take the air with Brancusi.'

You spoke of the modern and classic masters as if they were neighbours. Comrades who would lean over the fence and share a piece of fruit. They may have been long gone, but the core question that drove them throughout their journey was as relevant to you as the daily news.

In your novel *To the Wedding*, you created a narrator called Nikos Tsobanakos. A composite of my first name, your second name. Tsobanos is Greek for shepherd which in French is berger. Nikos Tsobanakos was an old time *rembete* – one of the last originals of the Greek 'blues' scene. I am sure I met someone exactly like him before we met.

In 1982 I went to Greece for the first time. I was drawn to the music of *rembetika*. But the old clubs had closed, and the new wave had not started. It was hard times once again for the *rembetes*. Nikos Tsobanakos had arrived in Athens in 1923. I found him hustling as a tour guide at the Akropolis.

He was conducting a tour for American tourists. I crept up beside him. He was wearing his dark English suit, and his cap was covered in marble dust. His body was stooped, like that of the Anafioti stonemasons, but he had an assuredness of the bounty that lay between the arc of his open hands. He had walked these paths many times before, and the soles of his soft rubber shoes were well worn. Finally, he had come to the regular marble bench where he delivered his flourish. With dry lips, one knee bent on the hard surface, shoulders hunched to hold his loose jacket, and with three quarters of his glance directed down to the Agora, and the other quarter holding the attention of the group he declared:

'Before you Ladies and Tzentelmen...this is where it all began.

'This! This is where they all came to meet. Zeus and Athena. Geometry and Philosophy. Socrates and that scoundrel Alcibiades. Architecture and Democracy.

'This is where you can find God on a scale that everyone can imagine, and a theatre in which the Gods can understand us, and a frame inside of which we can all forgive each other. This Ladies and Tzentelmen. This... This is where Civilisation began. Thank you!'

At the end of the day Nikos Tsobanakos would go back to his apartment in Neos Kosmos. As he entered, he placed his cap on the hook. Next to it hung his baglama.

Seeing it alone he felt contrite.

Each night he confessed: 'If I am going to tell lies, lies, and more lies for a few lousy drachmas, at least I should sing the ones that come from our life.'

John came to Athens ten years later. By then *rembetika* music had a rebirth and Nikos Tsobanakos was singing in a taverna called Nea

Smyrna. In a letter from the island of Simi you thanked me, for what I do not know, and you rejoiced in the apartment I led you to: 'where the soul takes a douche, and the balcony on which you eat like sailors at last returned – surrounded by the green hair of abandoned mermaids'. And you recalled the *rembete* voice 'white tolerant sharp-as-flint' and bitter-sweet like Turkish coffee. After the spiralling sequence of intense *zembekika* Nikos Tsobanakos would end the night with a slower *hasapiko*. A song first sung by a friend before the war.

Parting Goes on Hurting
For every pain and every sorrow a herb is found
But the sorrow of parting can never be healed.
Bitterness and torment disappear in time,
But the eyes you love are never forgotten.
Even if you go to a strange place to forget it,
You'll remember and cry for the hour you parted
My heart is sick from knowing only tears,
To love, to part, did you vow it to be so? (Holt: 99)

2. Going to John's House

Drrllp, drrlp, drr, pppp, shhhh, sh. The percolator dribbles its first full pot of coffee. Beverly launches her first cigarette with her light-blue Bic flick lighter. Pushkin the cat is sitting by the pot-bellied stove heater. Not moving. John comes trundling down the external stairs. They are steep and narrow. His frayed tartan slippers are barely gripping the wooden steps, and his white flannel gown is flapping in semaphore.

'Is Yves awake?'

Yves emerges from his bedroom in boxers and a Guns N' Roses t-shirt. First stretching his arms and then pulling in his little fists to rub the sleep away from his eyes. It is a cloudy Thursday morning outside.

'Yes Papa, I am here.'

The postman's yellow van has come early. The wheels gristle over the gravel, a handbrake is yanked, and the grumble of the diesel engine hovers in neutral.

Pushkin is annoyed. He abandons his silence and pitter-patters over the remaining ash and bark on the empty newspapers that had been laid to dry fresh logs on.

I go out to get more wood for the fire.

Up the hill seventeen cows chew with satisfaction. Louis has finished the morning milking. He has hung up the clusters of metal tubes and rubber teats. He is now dragging the steel churn into the boot of his Renault before he drives off to deposit it at the dairy. Louis is a peasant who owns the house in which John, Beverly and Yves lived. He is a bachelor and is a close friend to the family.

So how did I meet John Berger?

Towards the end of my doctoral candidature at Cambridge, Deborah Levy, who was the Trinity College writer-in-residence, invited me to dinner and sat me next to the distinguished Visiting Professor Teodor Shanin. Deborah informed me that he and I had a lot in common as he was the world authority on the sociology of peasants. However, she also instructed me not to go home until *after* he left. I dutifully chatted with Teodor, and at one point he asked the customary campus question: 'What is your dissertation about?'

I proceeded to give him a brief outline of my approach on the theme of exile in John's writing, but mostly I zeroed in on the theoretical problem that I had been trying to get my head around earlier that day. I had developed the habit of responding to this customary question by verbalising that day's work. In a rather obtuse way, I interwove speculations on John's books with reflections on the order in which theory and practice relate to each other.

Teodor was not impressed with my tangle of knots and snorted out: 'You make a friend of mine sound like he is dead!'

'He is your friend?' I asked with my jaw dropping.

I had no idea that Teodor and John were fellow members of the Amsterdam-based Transnational Institute, and that Teodor's work had influenced John's trilogy *Into Their Labours*, his collection of short stories and novels on peasant life. I later noticed that Teodor occupied the role of authoritative commentator in the documentary on *Pig Earth* directed by Mike Dibb. However, on that night, Teodor's comment was like a red rag to a young bull. I charged. He swerved and chuckled. Finally, Deborah had enough, and with tabouli in one hand and chicken in the other, she insisted that we change subject.

Teodor did not give up so easily. He invited me to continue the debate the following afternoon. When I inquired at the Porter's Lodge, for the room of the Visiting Professor I was directed to make a right at the main quad and head to the last room on the ground level.

'You could not miss it, as it is the old rooms of Sir Isaac Newton.'

When Teodor arrived at Trinity in his checked flannel shirt the porters sent him round the back as they assumed he was the new gardener. He wore a version of that flannel shirt all summer. It was his uniform. To show that he was at work he kept his sleeves rolled up and a Bic 4 Colours retractable pen in his chest pocket. In the winter he also wore it with the sleeves rolled up, but he added a white vest underneath.

I knocked on the heavy door. There was Teodor sitting behind a massive desk. He opened a bottle of Armenian cognac and we continued where we had left off the night before. Neither of us was giving ground on either the priority of theory or the primacy of personal experience. Suddenly, Teodor paused, picked up the phone, and thundered: 'Let's ring John!'

Fuck! He had Newton's room, the cognac, and the direct line to God. To my relief, it was John's partner Beverly who answered. She told Teodor that John was out for the day.

They made some giggling small talk, Teodor scribbled a number on a piece of paper, and after he hung up, he ordered me to ring John later that evening. As a former military commander, Teodor knew exactly how to issue orders.

I walked home, heading down the back lanes, passing the house of Clive James and across the fields of Jesus Commons. All along I was scratching my head, and when I got home, I scrambled to find as many gold coins as I could muster. That night I went to the nearby pay phone and rang a French number.

A delicate 'hello' answered.

I immediately went on a star-struck rant.

John interrupted with: 'Nikos, would you like to come and stay with us for a weekend?'

There was a sign in the graduate's common room of my college: 'If you have an idea, we will pay for it.' I approached my head tutor Professor Andy Holmes, and he issued the funds for a plane ticket to

Geneva. This was the first of many visits. Soon their home in Quincy was where I went for Christmas dinner. Every summer I would ride over on my old motorbike – a 1975 BMW Boxer.

It took some time to get the green light to focus my dissertation on John's writing. It was considered presumptuous and premature to write on a living author in Cambridge. In his laconic ways Tony Giddens, my supervisor, was eventually supportive. He rejected my original proposal of studying the literature by migrants in Australia.

'No one will take you seriously, Nikos.'

When I switched to a comparative study of celebrity exiled authors such as Nadine Gordimer and Milan Kundera, he picked up my hesitancy and recycled my auto-critique.

'Yeah, the connections between them will seem remote.'

'How about a focus on a single author, like John Berger?'

'That is much more manageable.'

When Tony promptly returned my draft chapters I noticed that the margins were littered with squiggles, dashes, and question marks. Not good I assumed. I asked him to decode these hieroglyphs.

'You need more structure, Nikos!'

'Aha, oh, and how do I add more structure?'

'Well Nikos, you add more rigour.'

'Okay, and how do I introduce more rigour?'

'By giving it more structure...'

I went round and round on this roundabout for a few years. I read everything I could find on and by John Berger.

Walking along Kings Parade I crossed paths with Tony's research assistant Graham McCann. Most of the dons coped with us pesky graduates by tilting their head to the other side and acting as if they were reciting Wordsworth. Graham smiled and told me that he had heard that I was working on John Berger.

‘My only problem is that John seems to write faster than I can read. Everywhere I turn I find something new.’

Graham nodded sympathetically and tightened the upturned collar on his James Dean coat.

‘I had a similar problem when I was writing on Raymond Williams. He was alive and prolific. I felt like a monkey trying to climb up a greasy pole. You need to draw the line somewhere.’

I concluded from this that what I needed was a guillotine. I needed to find a justifiable point and then make a hard cut. As we stamped to both warm our feet and mimic Tony’s gesture when he was making a key point in his lectures, I decided that the trilogy *Into Their Labours* was where I would stop. At that point only the first volume, *Pig Earth*, had been published.

‘There are two doors in life. From one you enter and by the other you leave.’ So sang the *rembete* Stelios Kazantzidis.

In Quincy the houses have four doors. Two at the front: one for the stable and the other for the residence. To the side is a large double gate, wide enough for carts to enter the barn. At the back is a rarely used entrance to the cellar. John’s house had been unoccupied for decades before he, Beverly and baby Yves entered. It also had a small garden in which they planted potatoes, herbs and flowers. Wild blueberries grew along the side of the house that avoided the long exposures to summer sun. Beverly kept a brown leather-bound notebook – when to plant? what order? how to rotate the vegetables? when to dig out the potatoes? They were lifted out in October. Louis picked his apples and pears in November. Then the snow would come.

My father knew the answer to all these questions. He also knew the value of a fallow period and the function of a copse. But he would not verbalise them, let alone write them down in a book. At the beginning of each spring, he would lean on his shovel and survey his suburban vegetable patch. He would whisper and point to the ground. 'This year the beans here, tomatoes there!'

What was wrong with me? Why did I not see that the history of his knowledge was in these decisions? I never followed any of his steps. As a young man all I wanted to do was flee from domesticity. My mother made sure I was chained to my desk, and she was not sparing with the chores in the kitchen. My dreams were far from the kitchen sink and vegetable garden.

The great philosopher Michel Serres was also the son of a peasant. His ancestors were farmers since neolithic times. He was the first to pick up the pen. He was aware of how far he had gone, but he was also conscious that his working methods were close to the ancestral uses of the land. He abhorred the total subjection of the land to rational industrial plans. It terrified him. The absence of gaps was suffocating: 'our wisdom was a margin, our being only a swerve. I was unaware that our wisdom lay in that little bushy grove, that humid low tract through which we wade awkwardly or that abandoned field with weeds and that little thicket of low bushes, all these deserted fields. I can breathe freely and fully in a field because it is bordered by brushwood full of quarrelling birds, because that field lies at the outskirts of a forest, marked by deserted areas, by spaces left fallow, badly tilled. Our wisdom consists of this negation, this disorder, this lack of culture.' (*Detachment*, 7) Serres claimed that his books had gaps, pauses, were never finished, they returned again and again to the same starting point, they swerved to produce new life, and in the words of his father, to 'leave some ears of wheat in the field for the gleaners'. (11)

In the past the peasants would live side by side with their animals. Separated by a wall, but their doors were identical. Since John had moved in no cows or pigs crossed the threshold. The stable had been converted into a *cave* – cellar. Pets were permitted in the house. Mamma cat had not been spayed. John had the grisly job of dispensing with the litter. Mamma cat stuck close to Beverly. One year a little white kitten with tiny black dots above his eyes came out. He started following me around. I named him Pushkin. John was forced to stay his execution. I think he liked hearing the name in the house. I talked to Pushkin with the surrealist expectation of a response. He maintained his ironic demeanour, and when I was done, would blithely turn away. Eventually, John recognised Pushkin as part of the family. He would sign his letters 'love from Quincy, Beverly, Pushkin, and Yves'. However, it was Beverly who put out the small bowls of leftovers. John thought feeding cats made them lazy. He claimed that there were plenty of marmots furrowing around the steep escarpment across the road from the house. It was from there that Yves would launch his fireworks every 14 July. Yves was born in the village, he became Louis's main helper, studied to become a painter in Geneva, and has lived all his life in Quincy. He had his mother's eyes and fair hair. At the age of three he fell off a wall, broke his nose, and has continued to look suitably rustic.

John had a little wooden ramp that he placed over the step to the *cave* as he parked his Honda. My Boxer liked being outside. John would routinely tap the chain of the bike to check for any slackness. I would unclip the cover of the carburettor to clear away any residual gunk in the petrol. Neither of us had any real idea of how our motorbikes worked.

My headlights went blank one day. John and I looked at each other and in sync we said:

'Oh!'

'*Quel désastre.*'

On the Richter scale of one to ten, we had no clue. After lunch we rode down to an old and chubby mechanic in Mieussy. Jacquard was in his blue overalls and steel-capped boots. The garage was dark and vintage parts were stacked in a random order on the wooden shelves. He smiled as he unscrewed the headlight ring, pulled out the old bulb and replaced it with a new one. He then refitted the cover and sealed it with black electrical tape.

'No charge.'

John and I looked on in awe. It could have been brain surgery.

The land on the side of John's house rose at a steep angle. From the road, the wide double doors opened so a cart could enter the vast barn. From the front of the house a steep metal staircase led to John and Beverly's bedroom. None of the doors were ever locked. In fact, I don't remember seeing any keys. Or wait, was there not a big key that sat at the bottom of the letterbox?

The house was behind a hairpin bend. Once you turned into the gravel path and parked in front of the verandah there was a feeling of shelter – like being tucked under the arm of a bigger friend.

When Yves and I played ping-pong in the barn we kept the double doors open. It lit the cathedral, and it was the only time we noticed traffic. Beverly mentioned that the Tour de France came close to the village one year. But apart from the postman the route was seldom used.

My grandmother's house was similar. Hariklia's two cows and horse slept below and the three rooms for her and the four children were above. There was a small barn to the side. In the courtyard there was an alcove with a trough for washing everything.

My grandmother was a refugee from a village near Trabzon on the Black Sea. Winters in Trabzon were sharp. The pine forests resembled the Swiss mountains. During the cold months a limbo set into the village. My great-grandfathers would cross the Black Sea and work in the granaries near Odessa. During these seasonal migrations the women assumed authority and the children were fatherless.

My grandmother was traumatised by the violence of wars and forced migration from Trabzon in Turkey to Kastoria, Greece. She would have witnessed slaughter, but more died on the journey from malaria. Throughout her life her mood ranged from suspicious to sceptical. In the village, she insisted on locking all her doors and windows. Whenever I stayed, she would put me in the ancient brass bed. Icicles formed under the eaves and hoarfrost condensed on the single-paned windows. The snowflakes would fizz on your tongue and rise to waist height. At night she would bury me under heavy blankets. She complained that she could never warm her feet: 'cold as sticks'. The solution was a hot ceramic tile wrapped in a towel and then she slept soundly on the divan by the Aga oven.

'Niko! I have such lovely dreams when you are in the house.'

My grandmother could neither read nor write. She dictated letters to neighbours and asked Lazaro her grandson to read the replies. She mumbled as she crocheted by the window of her kitchen. When she came to live with us in Melbourne she complained about the solitude.

'These suburbs are like cemeteries.'

Mum and Dad worked long hours. When my brother and I came home from school she would put her hand on her heart.

'Ah my melancholia is lifting.'

When the solitude pressed too hard, she raked the leaves in my mother's garden.

In her village the television was turned on late at night and she cursed the politicians and scoffed at the contestants on the game shows. When she picked a log for the Aga oven she examined it carefully. Then placed it in the belly accompanied with some well-chosen words. In the summer the oven was turned off. I opened the belly and found an aerogramme that my mother had sent a month earlier. Lazaro had read the messages to her. I imagine her thinking, 'What is the point of keeping another blue sheet of paper? Out!'

John and Beverly would also move their bedding around the house. Yves always slept in the small room off the kitchen. I usually stayed on the fold-out bed in the library at the back of the house. I was blessed with a good back. Their neighbour Louis Sauge would marvel as I pushed up the haystacks in the barn like a *taureau*. Sitting in the cabin of his tractor and with his flat cap at a slight angle he would greet me.

'Nikos *cheval*.'

When guests arrived, they were offered the upstairs bedroom. John and Beverly made themselves comfortable in the large room between the kitchen and the library. During the day, Beverly used this large room as an office, and this is where the temperamental fax lived. John wrote by hand upstairs in the bedroom and Beverly typed up the drafts in the office below.

In my grandmother's house there was one photograph of each of her children and grandchildren on the fridge door. As you entered there was a laminated cabinet. On top of it were embroidered doilies and a Byzantine icon of the Madonna and Christ with a light floating on oil. There was only one other image in the house: *The Angelus* (1857–1859) by Jean-François Millet. A grim scene of two peasants who have stopped to pray while clearing a potato field. Salvador Dalí insisted it was a funeral scene. It was also one of John's favourite paintings.

When I first arrived at Geneva airport John was waiting with Katya. John was relieved that his daughter was liberated from her timid Swiss boyfriend. She was now dating Orestis Andreadakis, a prominent film critic from Athens; John had wanted her to meet another Greek. It was the beginning of winter and John anticipated that I would be inadequately dressed to face the piercing air of the Alps. Before mounting his Honda, he dressed me in a Swedish army coat. Nothing could penetrate that! It was the same coat that he used as a mental map for describing the squatter's camp in his novel *King*. The sleeves, pockets and collar were references to different parts of the camp.

On the morning of the second day, while making coffee in his white dressing gown and tartan slippers, he asked if I had any questions for him. I told him that I had already spent three years reading all his early essays and books. After a while I had become so immersed in his style that I could recognise his metaphors before I saw his signature. His first contributions for the weekly *New Statesman* were unsigned. To me they stood out. They had the same fingerprints as his later work.

'I have also read so many of your interviews that I feel like I already have the answers to your biographical experiences and political influences.'

He threw his hands up in the air and yelled: 'Great! Let's put up the flag of freedom.'

It was damp and cold outside. I accompanied John as he ran some errands. We cooked together and he introduced me to his neighbours.

As I flew back to Cambridge, I realised that I got so much more from John than corrected facts and additional references. He had received me at the airport in his full leather outfit. In the morning he walked around with a white flannel gown which opened and closed around his thin calves. His greetings were warm and his chest and belly rotund. I was struck by his eyes. At once furtive and kind. Sparkling with curiosity but also intense in his focus when Louis spoke.

John was always very generous with his time and thoughts. He was willing to recall and acknowledge the influence of others. His own sense of how his books were connected was vague. His mind was not fixated on building a unified body of work. While there was a recurring pattern in his themes, he gained no pleasure in talking about himself. His energy was directed to the urgency of understanding the conflicts in the present. Turning attention back to his 'personal' achievement made him uncomfortable. When his friend the photographer Jean

Mohr proposed to do a book of portraits that he had taken of him John's reflex was to invite Jean to sit so that he could draw him. He didn't have the desire to position himself as an authorial figure either. When Jean pointed out that his book was about the process of friendship and aging, John relaxed.[3] There were very few mirrors in the house.

At a later visit to his house in Paris I asked John about the orientation of his imagination, and in particular his relationship to the wide range of subjects he had written about. I recalled Eric Clapton's reflections on the different bands he played in – he claimed that it was not so much that he left a band, but that he felt drawn by the inexorable energy of others, and I wondered about the oscillation across the borderline between the self and other. John responded to my question in an elliptical manner.

'Is it a borderline, or is it a process of osmosis? It seems to me, that as soon as you begin to think of writing about another being you begin to efface that border. You might then ask, where does the energy come from for the effacement of that border? I think that comes from what one has lived. That which has become part of one's experience and life already belongs to other people. If one wants to put it in a rather cheap aphorism: the self is already collective. That collective is made up of all the people with whom one has interacted positively or negatively, it is made up of pain and pleasure, of hope and fear, of security and risk. Think, for example, of how we dream, and in particular of how we dream of people, either of people who are dead but whom we knew, or people whom we once knew and are still alive. We say that they come back to us in our dreams, but what this means is that they are already in us. Writing about other people at the most primary and deep level, is about those who are already in us.'

John always stressed that writing about other people is an opportunity for the self to get beyond its own narcissistic fixation and follow the other's lead and could take you elsewhere. To illustrate the point while we were discussing this in Paris, he then read me a story that he had written just days earlier.

I am an alpine lake. I measure 750 metres by fifty metres. I am about seventy metres deep. One of my neighbours to the west is an alpage called Annely. I am called Falin. I reflect with my eyes shut. When I do this indiscriminately, you, you see dark green, nothing else. In my depths are arctic fish and a current that never stops. Men take photos but they never work because I keep my eyes shut. On my surface, flat stones when well thrown, ricochet. And whenever I am touched ripples of sensation are visible. The snow melts in May and June. In August when the sun is hot, Hunstein pours cool sand down my spine. The sun is high enough to reach only in the summer. And every summer Schafberg and his rockfaces tell the same story: it is the kind of story which is told when a crowd of people are drunk. According to this story I was once a fountain in a bath parlour, a hammam. After being massaged people came to place dice on low round stone tables arranged around me, sometimes they brought women to me. They gambled for whatever good they could see on this earth. One day a man lost everything he had and might have had. He was a God, and it is dangerous to let Gods lose. We've always known that. In his terror he lifted up the hammam and threw it on its side. The gambling tables rolled through the walls like millstones and have stayed there vertical ever since. Everybody fled. Nobody returned. The edge of the table cracked and crumbled. Grass grew where the dice once rolled. But in the summer, when the sun is in the right position, one can still see the gambling tables and the shepherds call them Hunstein. When I reflect indiscriminately with my eyes shut, the dark green you see may change in mid-afternoons to turquoise, and at dusk when the trout leap through my lids the turquoise becomes slate. In August kids row the length of me. But at other moments, concentrated by the pain of memory, eyes still shut, I reflect with discrimination. I reflect shadows, light, stone, sky, goat, pine, cows, rowing boat, man, face, moustache, earring, linen shirt, Hunstein diving, Schafberg floating on his back, grass grass grass, stars, a boy's zizi. People try to buy me in jewels, but I am never there, nor my sister Zamtisa. About her I cannot sing. But it happens to me sometimes, I open my eyes, when I do you fall into me, helpless.

John had an older and rugged neighbour called Angeline. Jokingly he referred to her as Ma. But not so jokingly she would scoff: 'Huh! Yes, well you're a writer and all writers are liars. There are no bigger liars in the world than writers. That's what you do, you go into that room and write down lies, don't you?'

During the 1990s I would visit my grandmother Hariklia every Easter. She lived in a village called Mesopotamia near the town of Kastoria in Greece. The entrance to my grandmother's house was five steps above the stable. It had a little verandah that was wide enough for a small coffee table and chair. In the morning, I would eat my slices of fresh bread with honey and then spend an hour or so doing some writing.

My aunt Nitsa walked by, saw me working, let out a huge sigh, and crossed herself more out of pity than respect:

'My God isn't your head already full! Aren't you tired from all these years at the desk?'

I wasn't tired. I had just finished my doctorate and I was bursting to start my academic career. For her, the idea of an education was that it put you in a place where you could afford to work less. What sort of progress do you call it when you end up carrying your work with you wherever you go! She thought all bookworms were a bit soft in the head, like her other nephew the village idiot. My aunt could not hide her confusion. For her writing was a chore, or even worse a form of punishment. It should be confined to either a solemn duty or a festive moment – such as letters to inform relatives of funerals and weddings. Writing was alien. The pleasure of communication was in stories, dancing and embroidery. If you had something to say, you did so with your mouth, body and needles. Why should a young man sit alone at his desk with a pen and paper? Those questions of life and death have no answers. The world is not on a page.

'God be with you, my son. But hurry up and finish. Go to the *plateia* – the square – where all the other young people are.'

At the beginning of my doctoral research, I asked my supervisor whether he thought I should try to interview John. In Australia I mixed more freely with artists and writers than other academics. In London I was already working for the artist-run journal *Third Text*. It felt like a normal next step to meet John. In a rather protective voice Tony responded: 'Ah Nikos, I don't think that would be necessary. After all I have written a lot of books on Marx, Weber and Durkheim and I never interviewed them.'

When I told Tony that I was flying out to Geneva to spend a weekend with John, Tony was thrilled. We were walking along the corridor in Free School Lane that joined Social and Political Science with Anthropology, and he announced to everyone: 'Nikos is going to meet John Berger!' Even the old curmudgeon Ernest Gellner was impressed. The relationship between the two schools was tense. A decade earlier a thin plaster wall had been put up between them. Now Tony needed the support of the anthropologists to elevate the status of sociology in the university's hierarchy. Gellner berated graduate students when they appeared late to his seminars, and enjoyed walking across the lawns that were exclusive to the senior fellows. Along with Tony giving away points in games of squash to the stooped professor, my impending encounter with John was used as a tiny token of reconciliation.

In Quincy I got close enough to John to see the cracks in his fingers. As he cut bread, I got a glimpse into how his nimble gestures connected to the way he made sense of things. Driving to Taninges he pulled over to admire a large tree. I appreciated the courtesy he showed to shopkeepers, and above all, the deep reverence he held for his friend, neighbour and the owner of his house, Louis Sauge.

I completed my PhD at the same time that Teodor ended his fellowship. He asked me if I would share the driving for his return to Manchester. I agreed. However, when I saw him reclining the driving seat as if it were a beach bed, I decided I had better drive the whole way. By Australian standards it was a short trip. At the end of the journey Teodor was determined that I begin my academic career in the Sociology Department at the University of Manchester.

The journey to Quincy usually began in rain. In Manchester it constantly rains. When it isn't raining it either drizzles or mizzles. Sometimes, when everything seems to be on a very, very brief pause, a sharper and dryer cold hovers, and then, as if by surprise, snow starts to fall. When it does snow the diffuse light that peers through the rain switches to amber. The flakes quiver in their descent. The cold snap rarely holds long enough for the snow to settle. When friends asked about the weather, I told them that it only rains between the beginning of July and the end of June. Making sure they got the point I would draw a circle in the air.

On the third trip to Quincy, Scott McQuire, my best friend from Melbourne, offered to accompany me on the bike. Scott, a world authority on photography, was keen to meet John, and an extra pair of long arms would be helpful in the barn.

The journey kept being delayed by the rain. On this occasion it was raining outright monkeys, and my end-of-semester cold was lingering. Scott pumped me up with echinacea and I bought him a waterproof suit. We loaded the side panniers and the saddle that sat over the fuel tank. I tucked his jacket in under his gloves and checked his helmet. The rain kept falling, but we set off for London. The motorway was sluggish, and I filtered between the lanes. Scott was gripping the handles on the back of the seat and his head, rising above mine, surveyed everything. He was too big and too curious to curl in and reduce the wind resistance. Riding with Scott was like a having a sail pulling behind you.

Just outside Birmingham we stopped for petrol. Scott finally tried to relax his grip, but his hands were heavy. As I turned, I realised that I had tucked his jacket sleeves under, not over his gloves, and the open parts were working like a funnel for the rain. His hands had been sitting in buckets of water. We laughed as we squeezed the gloves and held them under the hot-air hand dryers.

We stopped for the night in London. Simon McBurney and Lilo Baur had prepared dinner. Simon was the director of Théâtre de Complicité and Lilo, his partner, was the lead in their production of John's story 'The Three Lives of Lucie Cabrol'. Simon had bought a new blender which he had figured out was perfect for crushing ice, green apples and vodka. He played a recording of Mongolian throat music and gave a short dissertation on how it could be incorporated in his next theatre production.

We overslept the next morning. I did not want to miss the first ferry. We quickly clipped the panniers onto the back of the bike, jumped onto the A2 motorway and fanged it towards Dover. As we approached the port I dropped into a lower gear and cruised towards the front of queue. After boarding the ferry, I tied the bike to the bars on the side walls, and we went up for a late breakfast. Scott returned with two brandies. He was shivering.

'More from fear.'

I apologised and promised: 'The moment the bike rolls into France we will not ride on another motorway. It is village to village. The sun will shine. I will go slower. You will ride with the helmet open and smell everything. The coffee will be wonderful.'

Scott now insists that we did not have dinner with Simon and Lilo. He claims that the only time he met them was at my parents' house in Melbourne. Simon's group Théâtre de Complicité had been invited by the Melbourne Festival to stage *The Three Lives of Lucie Cabrol.* John told them to invite my parents. Requests from John were so rare that they were received like a fiat from Olympus. My parents countered by hosting a small BBQ for the cast and some of my friends. I am sure the latter half is true. I have a photo of everyone on my dad's back verandah. But I don't remember, as Scott insists, that our overnight stay in London involved getting drunk with Deborah Levy in a Turkish restaurant in Hackney.

Before John and Beverly moved to Quincy, they lived even higher up on the *alpage* at Roche Palud. At that height there is snow on the ground almost the whole year round. The house is now an exclusive chalet, but then it had a barn as big as an art school, no electricity, and it sat at an elevation of 1500 metres with a view from the outdoor bog that rivalled Ruskin's favourite. Every morning John would start the day by sitting there with the door open to the heavens.

When Beverly was pregnant with Yves they decided to move down the valley to Quincy. At that point there was even a small café in the village. They now had electricity, but John still had to disassemble the outhouse and empty the pit at least once a year.

A year before I met John, I had a lunch with Edward Said, the author of the magisterial *Orientalism* and the brilliant campaigner for Palestine. He talked with reverence about John's work and even more warmly about John. Edward had a voice that flowed like a river but would creak and leap when he hit a rocky point of injustice. He was tall, broad-shouldered, and looked impeccable in a dark suit. And then he added:

'But whatever you do don't go and visit him in the village, there are pigs and shit everywhere!'

'That's fine with me, it sounds like my father's village.'

It was the first time that the idea of visiting John in the village entered my head. At that point I was trying to work out the status of *Ways of Seeing* in my dissertation. I was given this book by my university friend Michael Healy. He was a poet who had just returned to Melbourne after a year in Berlin. In sympathy with my irritation at what Aby Warburg called the excessive empiricism and petty formalism of art history he sneaked a copy in his dungarees and walked out of the university bookshop. The moment I started reading it my mind blew up. At last, I thought, a real comrade in art and politics.

Talking to Edward Said about *Ways of Seeing* I confessed that having spent two years in the university library reading almost all of John's earlier essays I found the book to be more like an elegant distillation of multiple lines of thought. It was no longer a singular explosive event.

Edward Said carefully cut into his veal schnitzel and suggested: 'Insert that comment and move on.'

The book *Ways of Seeing*, published in 1972, started out as a four-part documentary for the BBC. John had a tiny budget but an outstanding team. It was shot mostly in a studio in Ealing that was adjacent to a railway line. Takes had to be timed during the intervals between the passing trains. On completion the series was screened late at night. It immediately developed a cult status and was re-screened regularly. The book that followed was designed to be cheap and accessible. The team were determined that it should be sold for less than one pound. It has been a bestseller ever since. No art, media or cultural studies student can complete their degree without, at some point, passing through the clarifying pages of this book. The book has been translated into countless languages and the TV series continues to be visited by millions on YouTube. The BBC still enjoys the handsome royalties whereas John and his team received a flat fee.

John first met Beverly when she was working for his publisher and was sent to promote *Ways of Seeing* at the Frankfurt Book Fair. Beverly had refined features and beautiful eyes. She would look elegant in silk scarves. I recall that, in a photograph with the pipe-smoking publisher Victor Gollancz, she held her cigarette with pride and composure. She recalled that John did not even possess copies of his own books. If someone expressed appreciation of any of John's possessions his reflex reaction was to give it to them. Beverly felt compelled to buy at least one copy of each of his books and then stored them in a secret built-in cupboard. This collection, which now includes all the translations of his books, has migrated to the archive in the converted pigsty that sits opposite the house. Beverly also made sure that John's essays were dispatched to publishing outlets in London, Stockholm, Hamburg, Paris, Madrid, Mexico City and Istanbul. Her grandfather was the Bancroft who was the main philanthropist to UC Berkeley, and the main highway leading to the campus is named after him. She was content in the village house. She loved the garden vegetables and wild blackberries. When Yves emptied the dishwashing machine, she would tenderly exclaim 'my son'. Beverly was the initiator and keeper of John's archive.

My father always said that clothes made of expensive material turn out to be cheaper, and you should not look to save money when shopping for food. John was the same. He had no idea about fashion but loved the cashmere scarf I once wrapped around his neck. After a successful treatment for his sore back John took Yves and me to the most expensive restaurant on the hillside facing Geneva. We were on motorbikes. The blue-rinse ladies who were dining had their chauffeurs waiting outside. The fish was extraordinary, the waiters laughed a bit too loud at all our jokes, and as we left, they presented our bike helmets in a ceremonial manner that was fit for royalty.

I once asked John why he never bought the house in Quincy from Louis. He was clearly very attached to it. His desk was upstairs by the window at the end of the bedroom. On this small table was a checked tablecloth, with just room enough for a couple of A4 sheets, an Indian ink bottle and another book. He used a Sheaffer fountain pen. Yves pointed out to me that Schäfer in German means shepherd, which of course in French is Berger. In the kitchen there was a pot-belly stove with a long pipe that kept the room cosy in the winter. The wood was stored under the verandah. They even installed a hot shower decorated with the odd Delft tiles.

So why didn't they buy it?

John replied: 'I have no wish to. This predisposition in myself – because it is almost a repugnance – served me very well in my relationship with the peasants who are my neighbours. I have noticed that whenever a peasant sells his house to say a Swiss family so that they can use it as a holiday home, and no matter whether it is a fair price, there is always a lament in the contract; the peasant feels as if he has betrayed his ancestors. It is felt as the illegitimate taking of something that if justice existed belonged to them.'

He then recalled an incident when a family was short of money and was forced to break off a portion of their land to cover the expense of a wedding.

'They sold it to the groom's family with the right to repurchase. A transaction had taken place. Money had changed hands, but it was as if the land was not alienated.'

When the Global Financial Crisis hit Greece property prices

plummeted. I had been thinking for years of owning a house there. My friends urged me on.

'It will be good for you to have a base, and it will help all of us.'

John's words haunted me.

'But it feels like stealing!'

I waited for things to settle. Ten years later, on the advice of Yanis Varoufakis, who was then the finance minister in Greece, and his partner Danae Stratou, an artist and unofficial ambassador of the island of Aegina, I made an offer on a little house and land with 100 pistachio trees. As we were about to make the legal settlement Covid struck, and the Aussie dollar tanked.

I rang the owner Spyro and explained the drastic depreciation of my funds.

'Don't worry. Don't worry. We will do this in the old ways. You made a fair offer and I have received your deposit. We can complete the rest in good time.'

He waited an extra three months. The currency returned to its normal rate. Spyro continued to tend to the trees and harvest the nuts. We became friends.

Not long before I arrived in Quincy, John's chimney caught fire and the house almost burnt down: 'It was a question of two minutes. Had it not been for all the neighbours who came with water the whole thing would have gone. As it happens the damage was not very great. Knowing that Louis would hear about it very quickly via bush telegraph, I immediately went to tell him. His reply was "Well as long as you are fine, it's all right." A couple of months later I went around to pay the rent which he refused to accept. "No. I don't want it. You use the money to buy the things of yours that were burnt".'

I don't want to give the impression that John and the peasants had a monk-like disregard for material possessions. Artists, especially photographers, often gifted their work to him. Anya Bostock had the perspicacity to keep the painting by Fernand Léger when they separated. John treated each piece with great care and attention. As he stared deep into an image he would sigh, rub his thumb and index finger together, then an insight would flash in his eyes, and finally, a string of metaphors and similes would tumble out.

In the house in Quincy there were very few images that adorned the walls. There was an enigmatic poster of the pregnant Madonna by Piero della Francesca (*Madonna del Parto* 1460) that was glued into the arch under the verandah. The original painting was a fresco for the modest chapel of Santa Maria di Momentana. It showed the Madonna, patron saint of pregnant women, in a long flowing blue gown. Her hand is resting on her protruding belly. There is a slit in her gown revealing a cream-coloured under-dress. Two angels, one on each side of the Madonna, are holding up a damask canopy. The arching of the curtains draws the eye to her delicate and bent fingers that touch the slit. The poster was still legible even as it had peeled and faded in the harsh weather.

Inside the house there was another poster that was loosely framed, tinged in nicotine-time and watermarked, as if it had once served as a table protector. It was dedicated to Orlando Letelier, the Minister of Defence in the Allende Socialist government of Chile. The photograph shows him being frogmarched by a dozen armed soldiers. Their guns pointing at his back and their helmets shining in the morning sun. Orlando is in a dark suit, flared trousers, white shirt, with a wide floral tie. His head is upright, and his moustache is unflinching. The prison guards tortured this guitar-playing minister by breaking his fingers. A year later he was released. Soon after he was appointed as Director of the Transnational Institute where John and Teodor Shanin were research fellows. He continued to call for the downfall of the Chilean junta. The military ordered his assassination. His car in Washington

DC was detonated by Cuban exiles. Below the poster is a poem by John about the quiet valour of this man. It ends with an invitation to come to the village:

He has come
as the season turns
at the moment of the blood red rowanberry
he endured the time without seasons
which belongs to the torturers
he will be here too
in the spring
every spring
until the seasons returning
explode
in Santiago

– John Berger, Sept. 1976

The television was stored somewhere in the *cave.* It was rolled out for special events, and even then, it was placed at the end of the table, which meant you had to twist your neck as you do when checking for oncoming traffic in a tight intersection. In the kitchen there was also a barometer that only John believed in. He would hang his most recent charcoal drawing near the coat rack. Yves's room was full of punk and heavy metal posters.

Michael, John's younger brother, came for a lunch one day. He needled John about his lack of sentimental attachments.

Their father Stanley had served in the trenches for four years. Before the war he was intending to become a Catholic priest; after, he was emotionally shattered.

John stood up from the kitchen table, put his hand directly above his head, where a shelf ran along the old fireplace, and pulled down an antique compass that sat next to an old lantern.

'This compass was in Dad's pocket throughout the First World War. I can still feel the heat of his body.'

John was rough with books. He was impatient with scholarly entries in art catalogues and derisive towards academic books that were trapped in the intestines of theory. He could be overly enthusiastic about a friend's novel. Passionate hyperbole came gushing out. 'This is the first book to give rumour a form, to show how life in the margins is lived.' To advance a cause he could become a *partizano* for a book.

While he was thinking and writing he liked to shuffle quotes and images. If he needed an illustration, he would gladly trundle down the stairs, find the picture in his library, and cut it out. Even when he was engrossed in a book, he pencilled comments in the margins. Thoughts were most complete when used in conversation. A point well made in the kitchen or on the stage was the ultimate triumph. Books helped him go places. His life was guided by books, and he could see quickly how ideas could be shaped into a book. But he did not live in books, each book was a station.

There were no books in my house when I was child. At the age of four most of the lodgers in my parents' house had moved out. I was given my own bedroom. Along one wall were built-in cupboards that were mostly empty. I climbed up a chair and opened the top panel. In the darkness of the corner was a small blue hardback book. My hands reached in but could not clutch it.

'Baba, there is a book in my room, can you get it down for me.'

'Eat all your dinner, and then I will.'

There was a large plate of spinach, rice and feta cheese before me. I liked rice and didn't mind the feta. But how was I going to eat the spinach? It was all so slippery and made your teeth feel furry. I pinched my nose and gulped it down. My mother was speechless. I was a fussy eater. The only vegetables she saw me eat were potatoes.

Baba went straight to my room. I pointed to the cupboard, and he delivered my prize. He did not open it or ask any questions. I held it in my hands, and he walked out of the room.

It was an academic book on the theories of knowledge. It had a musty smell. A few diagrams but no images, and so many words that made no sense to me. It was exactly the book that John would toss away. The cover was rippled hard cardboard. I still have it in my library.

My mother started buying me books. I loved geography and science books. I could stare at maps of empires and only see the glory of travel. I was fascinated by volcanoes and how magma came from the deep. Then I read that one day the sun will explode, and I burst into tears.

'Why are you crying, Niko?'

'Mama, the sun will die in a million years.'

'Don't worry about that. You will be dead by then.'

'But what about my children?'

Other books came into the house. I bought a box full of *Reader's Digests* from the school fete for less than $2. The stall holder was happy to take whatever coins were in my hand. There was a second-hand bookshop in Chapel Street where I bought James Bond novels, and when a new bookstore opened, I thought I should get the Penguin edition of Plato's *The Republic*. The bearded owner thought it was a rather serious purchase. I acted as if I knew.

My mother loved to see me reading but that was no excuse for dodging domestic work. On Saturday mornings I would lie in bed with the doona up to my head and my nose in Mario Puzo's *The Godfather*. She came in with the vacuum cleaner blasting and pulled the covers away.

I would go to the library to escape housework. A row of books on a shelf was one of the most beautiful sights in the world. Each book a passport, together in a row, a dazzling mosaic. It was books that took me places.

3. Charisma as Giving

John's daughter Katya met Orestis Andreadakis in the dark. They were both film critics attending the Cannes Film Festival. John visited Katya in Athens while she was pregnant. One night, Orestis took John to a tavern where *rembetika* was being played. John was spellbound.

On his return to Quincy, John asked me to send him some information about the Greek Blues. I made a cassette and sent my copy of *Road to Rembetika*. He played that cassette many times, read the book carefully, and in the margins, he lightly pencilled his preferences of the lyrics to some of the songs. He was deeply moved by the rasping voices in the *rembetika* songs. He said that it reminded him of *Bone Machine* by Tom Waits. When I returned to the village, we talked a bit. One evening I danced to a classic *rembete* song called 'Cloudy Sunday'. He joined in by raising his arms and moving like a big bear.

That was the sum total of the information that he received.

In 1995 John wrote a novel called *To the Wedding*. It is the tragic story of a young vibrant woman called Ninon. She had contracted AIDS and then falls in love. Her father Jean travels along the Po River on his motorbike to attend the celebration of her wedding. John wrote *To the Wedding* from the perspective of a blind narrator – the *rembete* called Nikos Tsobanakos. I have a photocopy of an early draft that was still called *Last Friday Drives Monday Crazy: A Tama*. John had seen the *tama*, votives that hang off icons, in Greek churches. I must have read the draft to check the spelling of Greek names and instruments like the bouzouki and the baglama. Early in the novel he described a man doing the *zembekiko* dance.

'When you dance to a rembetiko song, you step into the circle of the music and the rhythm is like a round cage with bars, and there you dance before the man or woman who once lived the song. You dance a tribute to their sorrow which the music is throwing out.

Drive Death out of the yard
So I don't have to meet him.
And the clock on the wall
Leads the funeral dirge.
Listening night after night to rembetika is like being tattooed.'

Everything about the music of *rembetika* and the *zembekiko* dance is distilled in this brief passage. The dance is what Zorba danced in Kazantzakis's novel. In the film by Michael Cacoyannis, they changed the dance to the *syrtaki*. The Zembeks were irregular militia from Asia Minor. The men danced with their arms spread out wide like an eagle and their eyes facing their enemy. In the dance the eruptive splendour of youth and the infinite darkness of death are coupled. It invites the dancer to roll the dice with life. Zorba insists that the dancer does not hesitate, he is immortal, at one with God. For Zorba, God was neither an alien, nor an abstraction: 'I think of God as being exactly like me. Only bigger, stronger, crazier.' When Zorba danced his feet bounced on the ground. The earth trembled as if it were the skin of the drum.

If you think his receptivity of the essence of *rembetika* was a fluke, then consider the impact of his insights in a range of other fields.

In the early 1950s John was an art critic for the *New Statesman* and *New Society* as well as writing regularly for other progressive publications. He was never comfortable with that role, but as he said: 'At least it wasn't as bad as being a dealer or even worse, a pain-in-the-arse connoisseur.'

In 1966 John wrote an essay called 'The Historical Function of the Museum' in which he predicted that museums would no longer be confined to places for preserving precious objects and overseen by snobbish connoisseurs. On the contrary, the museum should connect to the energies of the street and become an open school.

In 2012 I forwarded this essay to Hans Ulrich Obrist, the Swiss artistic director of the Serpentine Gallery in London, and currently the most influential person in the art world. Obrist replied by describing the essay as the most 'amazing telepathy'.

John's most prophetic essay was 'The Moment of Cubism', published in 1967 in the *New Left Review*. In Cubism he saw the most vital synthesis of scientific discovery, political aspiration and aesthetic innovation. It was an epochal shift as monumental as the leap forward that was made in the Renaissance. John stressed that Picasso and Braque were not just depicting change, they were painting into a space he called 'interjacency'. They were incorporating the viewpoint of a field rather than adopting a specific vantage point and following linear perspective. They had grasped the significance of Cezanne's insights into the multiplicities of nature. They were alert to the vibrancy of new media. They saw the fragmentation of subjectivity and strived for new unities. They embodied a kinaesthetic approach to creation. Whether it is Gestalt psychology or Bourdieu's sociological theory of the *habitus*, the concept of the field has now expanded our understanding of the role of context.

In 1968 John sent a message to the novelist Mulk Raj Anand who organised the first edition of Triennale India. It is a brief note of solidarity with those who were committed 'to escaping from and even overthrowing' the 'disastrous legacy of imperialism'. He goes on to link the struggles in modern art with political projects and personal feelings. Recently, the outstanding writer and curator of contemporary art Nancy Adajania fastened onto this little correspondence and declared that this was a precursor of the 'globalism before globalism'.

Towards the end of his life John visited Ramallah and Gaza, cities that he named as the world's largest prison. On 13 January 2003 Multiplicity, the Italian collective of artists, architects and writers, followed a person with an Israeli passport from Kiryat Arba to

Kudmin. The next day they accompanied a person with a Palestinian passport from Hebron to Nablus. The two routes start and end at the same latitudes. The Israelis travelled through a series of expressways and tunnels. The Palestinians were detained at multiple checkpoints, diverted by walls, and forced to change transportation. Assuming all goes well, and the humiliation and harm is kept to a minimum, the journey of the Palestinian is five times longer than the Israeli's. Part of John's ancestry is Jewish. His grandfather was a Jew from Trieste. Stanley, his father, had converted from Judaism before the First World War. Contemplating the images of the bombings drawn by Palestinian children and the words of flight in the poems by Mahmoud Darwish, John wrote several testimonial essays which, as the scholar Juman Simaan noted, stood up like a martyr, an 'olive tree'. There is one drawing by John that haunts me. It has a narcissus flower blooming in the middle. There are a few olive-green streaks along the stamen and underlying the word 'her'. Surrounding this bare and bold flower are quotes from Darwish and stanzas written by John himself. The flower is surrounded by the contradictions of love and politics. He made this drawing while standing beside the grave of Darwish, who had died only days before.

John had an uncanny gift for metaphors. He was always drawn to the experiences of the marginalised, the persecuted and the uprooted. In his 1972 acceptance speech of the Booker Prize for his novel *G* he famously denounced the award-giving institution for benefitting from the historical crimes of slavery. He announced that he would share half of the £5000 prize money with the Black Panthers in London, and the rest would be used to finance the research for his next project, *A Seventh Man*, a book that would be focused on the migration of the peasants from the south of Europe to the industrial north.

The Black Panthers accepted the gift and used it to purchase a large terrace house in North London. The screenwriter Farrukh Dhondy told me that the place was used more for debating than planning an insurrection.

'The discourse was going well.' He chuckled.

'Until one night, a crazed man, armed with an axe and a machete knife, came screaming down the stairs. Everyone else legged it.'

The house was abandoned, and the revolution never happened.

John's book *A Seventh Man* was a pioneering study of the psychology and social experience of the peasant migrants. It is an unparalleled masterpiece. John, and his friend the Swiss photographer Jean Mohr, retraced the journey of peasants from their villages to the cities. He sat among the men in the village cafés and listened to stories that one cousin told another. John and Jean followed the trail of men carrying scuffed suitcases at train stations. They recorded the callous medical inspectors and customs officers as they processed the *Gastarbeiter*. He concluded that the journey was provoked by privation and inspired by rumours. He told the story from the point of view of a migrant's eye:

> In a dream the dreamer wills, acts, reacts, speaks, and yet submits to the unfolding of a story which he scarcely influences. The dream happens to him. Afterwards he may ask another to interpret it. But sometimes a dreamer tries to break his dream by deliberately waking himself up. This book represents such an intention within a dream which the subject of the book and each of us is dreaming.

A Seventh Man, like almost all of John's books, has been translated into many languages. When my mother read it in Greek she sighed: 'How did he know our lives? The book is so close to my experience as a migrant. It was like he was riding on my shoulder and lived inside my head!' It is the book that John felt revealed the most about him.

John's empathy extended to animals. He noted that zoos gained ascendency with industrial capitalism. Animals in cages were both a symbol of alienation from nature, and a source of wonder. The film theorist Barbara Creed and contemporary visual artist Joan Jonas have both recently turned to face the question of how we relate to animals, and acknowledged that their guide was John's short essay 'Looking at Animals'.

Sitting by the window of the living room in Paris I was caught between the density of garden outside and the volume of books and paintings on the walls. I asked John, 'How is it possible that you have written with such insight and elegance on so many different topics?'

I told him of a short piece I found in a 1950 issue of *New Statesman*.

'How did you know it was mine? I was not allowed to sign my pieces in those days.'

'Your metaphors stood out like thumbprints,' I replied.

I then asked about the role of metaphor and the imagination.

'Was this way of seeing and writing always in you, or did it come from outside? Or was it a constant oscillation between analysis and projection, a way of zooming in, and then flying out?'

John responded by reflecting on his time as a journalist. He highlighted the rituals of hospitality and the willingness to receive what is there.

When you are writing for a newspaper the first thing that you know is that you only have so many inches, and you have to arrange what you have to say within that space. If you don't, then your copy will be edited more than ever and therefore distorted. The elegance that you talk about, if there was an elegance, comes from the need to seize that space and arrange it exactly like you arrange furniture in a room. Before I started writing, I would have in my mind a small number of key metaphors which were the principal bits of furniture. I would arrange them to fit that space and make that space as hospitable as possible. Then I would write. Maybe I would write badly, and I would change things. It could take all day to write 250 words. But I would change in trying to get closer, as close as possible to that first ground plan of the given space. Then, if we continue with this image of the room or the house, you might ask whose room, or whose house? In a sense it was my room and my house because it was I who was arranging, but the way that I arranged it was to make it the room of the work, or the house of the artist I was writing about. That would be true of about nine tenths of what I wrote, and it was true even if I was negatively critical of a work or an artist. The one tenth when it wasn't true was when I wanted to attack something ferociously. Then probably, the room belonged to my anger and the result was not very good writing, because anger, although it is sometimes justified, has within it its own spiral of egocentricity.

Everyone dreams of a doctor that understands your body and your soul. Understanding is the torch that opens the way for care.

John's portrait of John Sassall (John Eskell), the country doctor in *A Fortunate Man,* is as close to reality as this fantasy permits. Sassall was perceptive and empathic. Dutiful and discrete. Sassall was John's doctor when he lived in the Forest of Dean – the ancient woodlands that border Wales. In one of Sassall's diary entries he produced a pithy and complete portrait of John:

He listens to everyone no matter what their station in life. He is interested in a peasant as he is interested in an intellectual. He always wants to be very accurate in his replies to any question you put to him. He pauses for quite a long time and eventually comes out with a very definite answer which is strictly truthful. He is never afraid of saying that he doesn't know or doesn't understand. He considers making love to be the most worthwhile thing in life. He is a nervous man in the sense of being highly sensitive to his surroundings, but he is not nervous in a neurotic way. He is very conscious of everything that goes on around him. He disciplines himself to write so many hours a day and does a lot of research in the Public Libraries, and he has the famous 1911 edition of the *Encyclopaedia Britannica* which he reads avidly. Always consistent in his polemical arguments. Against 'the System' in Russia particularly concerning Writers, Painters, Sculptors... Always extremely polite and gentle. Occasional severe temper-tantrums, mainly concerning domestic situations. (Quoted in Sperling: 9)

John had a profound respect for doctors. He admired anyone who could use their skill for the care of others. The nearest doctor to Quincy was called Michel. He had silky blond hair, an all-year tan, piercing blue eyes and a very delicate demeanour. We made social visits a few times in the summer period. Michel invited us to swim in the family pool. Yves and I would clown around doing bombs. John relaxing into his dogpaddling laps.

In most groups it was John that was the most attentive listener. However, in the doctor's house John talked the most. Michel enjoyed listening while adjusting his pipe. He basked in the pleasure of watching us swim, and he was a master at probing. Over lunch I noticed that when Michel spoke, John would move closer, right to the edge of his seat, as if poised to stand.

Michel and Sassall both wore glasses. In a rural setting that feature alone was enough to distinguish them. It was common for young doctors with socialist ideals to start their careers in the countryside. However, peasants were difficult patients. They were suspicious of *everyone* from the city. Peasants would listen to their doctor. They could hear his 'reasoning', but they also felt that even with his glasses the doctor could not see that 'life itself was mad' (*Once in Europa*: 10). As Sassall and Michel got closer to their patients neither lost their idealism. They became more tempered and reserved. With proximity they recognised both the strength of rural people and accepted their sheer irrationality. They would look at the body of their patients as if it were a landscape with nasty bumps and hidden recesses. They learned to hold back on extolling the progress of science and instead would read the contours of their bodies with their soft hands.

My mother took my index finger and ran it along her shin. I was a child and we had been snuggling under the blanket. I recoiled and almost fell out of bed. The bone was not smooth and straight. It was notched and dented. She laughed and explained how often she nicked herself with the sickle while harvesting in the fields. They would get up before dawn to go and harvest the tobacco, which was their cash crop, but in the heat of the day they would also work in the vegetable gardens.

My mother's father was killed during the Civil War. Her uncle Simeon fell into a deep period of grief. In the evenings after a drink at the *kafenion* he would stop at my mother's house and shout out.

'Nitsa! Where are you? *Ella do skato*. You little shit. Come here and give me a hug.'

His eyes glistened as he squeezed her good night.

When they harvested the wheat fields, Simeon kept an eye on my mother and her brother Nikiforo. My uncle Nikiforo was the same age as but even stronger than Simeon's sons. He had long arms, but Simeon feared that he had inherited his brother's weak back. In his grief he felt more pity for his brother's children than his own. As the sun approached noon, he would send Nikiforo to fetch water from the well. The walk along the shaded path was a respite.

After the publication of *A Fortunate Man* Sassall enjoyed a period of fame. The book was published at the time of the thawing of professionals. Several medical schools in Britain included the book in their curriculum. Young trainee doctors made their way to the Forest of Dean to learn from Sassall. They wanted to witness the example of his companionship with his patients – to emulate his touch and absorb the way he allowed kindness and knowledge to feed each other.

John told me that Sassall welcomed this attention as an extension of his pastoral role. However, Sassall also took stock, and reflected on the one aspect of his life that was sterile. He had married early in life, and the marriage remained a quiet but cold expression of obligation. John told me that he eventually divorced. I have since read that his wife died. Soon after, Sassall fell in love. It was a kind of love that Sassall had never previously experienced. John said that along with Sassall's usual laser-like focus, his eyes suddenly radiated an emerald happiness. On the day of his marriage Sassall locked the door to his study, sat behind the mahogany desk, and shot himself.

'This suicide was a total mystery to me!' said John.

I also could not fathom what abyss Sassall had fallen into on that day.

'Maybe the passion was too much for him. For a man who had focused so much on the care for others, that this sudden outburst of love – totally inside and all around him – must have felt like a solar eclipse. An explosion that was too intense, too close to the abyss. Maybe this proximity of love with the darkness of death felt too close together and too hard to keep apart.'

'Maybe,' John replied.

John had known Sassall for some time before he wrote the book about him. John was not trained in ethnographic research techniques, but as a journalist and a writer he had already refined the skill of looking and listening with care. His best writing came from passing his thoughts through the prism of other lives. *A Fortunate Man* was also the first collaboration that he undertook with the Swiss photographer Jean Mohr. They moved into separate rooms at Sassall's house. For two weeks they quietly followed the doctor on his day-to-day duties.

The following book *A Seventh Man* had a similar methodology. Forensic accountants always say follow the money. John and Jean followed their subject. It might sound obvious now, but at that time ethnographers focused on single sites and sociologists tracked the domination of structures. It was years before we started to train scholars in mobile methods.

Even when you know someone very well, it does not mean that they would want to share their pain and dreams. My grandmother was a refugee. While I lived in England, I would visit her at Easter in northern Greece. I would always ask her about her childhood in the Pontus region of the Ottoman Empire, on the southern coast of the Black Sea. She would wave her hand in the air as if swatting a fly, continue with her embroidery, and with a deep frown, declare: 'You are going to university. You have important books to read. You can't waste time talking to illiterates about the past.'

One day she asked where I had been all afternoon. I told her I was talking to Mihali in the *kafenion*.

'Why do you listen to that old cuckoo?'

'He was telling me stories about the village in Pontus and the difficult journey from Pontus to this village. I had no idea that so many people died from malaria.'

'He tells lies and makes up stories. That is not what happened.'

Out of an obligation to correct the old fool, she talked about her own journey, how tightly she held her mother's hand, how she got on a ship for the first time in her life, how they spent months in quarantine in the marshes outside of Thessaloniki, how they followed camels to the village where she now lived, and how peacefully they shared the house with the Muslim family before that kind family were sent to live in Turkey.

I decided to go back to the *kafenion* the next day and talk to more of the old men. On returning home each evening my grandmother would be baited, and she would add her own version of events.

The Mexican curator Cuauhtémoc Medina and I agree on many things, but when we first met at an exhibition in Helsinki, there were two points that instantly bonded us: the sadomasochism of travelling long haul in economy, and the wisdom of the iconic contemporary artist Jimmie Durham. Agreeing on the status of Jimmie is like an admission into a shared secret. Jimmie is taciturn. However, when he warms to you, each word he shares with you is like a precious mineral. I instantly felt an affection for Cuauhtémoc. We have met on only a few occasions. Each time we pick up words as if the gulf of time and distance made no difference. Cuauhtémoc's laughter is irresistible. In Mexico City he introduced me to the pleasures of eating fried and live insects. I stuck to the former. As one of the live ones crawled out of his mouth, he would whip out his tongue to pull it back in. Then he would laugh again as the 'gringos', at the table next to us, looked on in horror. First impressions can be fickle, but in this instance, I think I was unreasonably right.

Jimmie was going to be in Geneva the day I was scheduled to depart after a Christmas break at Quincy. I arranged a lunch so that John and Jimmie could meet.

Jimmie had a rough life. His family moved between Arkansas, Oklahoma and Texas in search of work. He had little formal education, picked up a bit about mechanics, brawled around and read poetry in bars with Marlon Brando. During the Vietnam War he was given the option – either do jail time or work as a code talker in the US Navy. There was a long tradition of using the Cherokee language to transmit messages on the radio. After serving his time in the war he returned to Texas where he met a Swiss couple whose parting words were:

'If you are ever in Europe, give us a call.'

He kept their number, and then when the ship docked, he went to the nearest payphone and dialled.

'Where are you, Jimmie?'

'I am in Rotterdam, Europe.'

'Don't move, we are on our way.'

Two days later Jimmie found himself in Geneva. By the end of the week, he was enrolled at the *école migre*. Finally, he felt like he was about to begin his introduction to Western Civilisation. Within a year he was admitted to the *École Supérieure des Beaux-Artes*.

Returning to the USA Jimmie began to work with the American Indian Movement (AIM). He was active at the conflict zone of Wounded Knee and served as a representative in the UN delegations. With his new knowledge of French, he could negotiate in Geneva. On behalf of AIM he also tried to broker partnerships with Third World leaders who, he discovered, were reluctant to welcome AIM in fear of encouraging 'their' own indigenous people and undermining their nascent nation-building efforts.

In the 1980s Jimmie dedicated himself to writing and sculpture. He had a show at Matt's Gallery in London, and we met soon after at the advisory meetings for the journal *Third Text*. After dinner we played a game: describe your *least* favourite animal.

When it came to my turn, I confessed to feeling repulsion at the sight of vultures in India.

'There was this vulture, long beak, scruffy feathers and protruding pink neck. It was picking away at the carcass of the cow that it had lifted onto the boughs of a tree.'

Jimmie was sitting quietly next to me.

'No, no, Nikos. Vultures are the most wonderful birds.'

'How is that?'

'First, they don't kill anything. And second, they are so much fun.'

To which I replied: 'Okay, I accept they are not birds of prey, but how do you have fun with a vulture?'

'Well, when I was a little boy, my grandfather would take me up the mountain, and we would lie on the ground. He would say, "Now

Jimmie, be really still." When the vultures came down, he would whisper, "Now Jimmie, act dead." And just as they got to the tips of our toes, we would jump up, pull funny faces and laugh loudly.'

Jimmie and his partner, the Brazilian artist/activist Maria Thereza Alves, moved from New York to Mexico, then from Dublin to Brussels, finally from Rome to Berlin. By the late 1990s he was in demand, and he could now finally afford to go to a dentist. In Sydney he participated in the Biennale, and I invited him to dinner at a Serbian restaurant. He tried to arm wrestle me for the bill, but his friend, the Indigenous Aunty Miriam that had travelled from Australia to fight with him at Wounded Knee, intervened.

'Jimmie, he wants to treat you, because you have come to his part of the world.'

Those were affirming words.

When John and Jimmie met it was a dark and cloudy day. The room had heavy curtains and the conversation was serious. Jimmie was wry and thoughtful. Although normally taciturn, Jimmie was leading the way.

John was following him like a country road. After lunch John drove me to the airport. As we neared the terminal he shuffled in his seat, scratched his head, ran his index finger along the upholstery on the roof of the car, and declared:

'The man is clearly a legend!'

When he pulled up in a parking bay John left the keys in the ignition. He thought the Swiss were too timid and even worse, they were also just too plain dim to steal. For him there was no light in the city of Calvin. It was starched in secrets. Secluded in a realm of apperception. As far as he was concerned the only major concern in Switzerland was boredom. Whenever he uttered the name Geneva it was with contempt.

There was not enough time that day. Or at least we needed to be in a different city. We all needed longer. I wished we were in Quincy. Jimmie would slope into the kitchen. Place his hat on the rack. I would fetch another bottle of Beaujolais from John's musty *cave*, which, even in the summer, is so cold that it ages your nostrils. We needed a different sky, or at least to sit beneath one of Jimmie's much-favoured linden trees.

Stephen Snoddy, the former curator at the Cornerhouse Gallery in Manchester, commissioned me to write a pamphlet on the challenges posed by artists from non-Western backgrounds to contemporary art. In this short book I contrasted the demands by contemporary Indigenous artists with the institutional efforts to accommodate their art within the troubled categories of 'primitivism'. At the launch of this publication Stephen turned to me. 'I appreciate your polemic but how would you curate an exhibition with artists from different parts of the world?'

'Not by repeating the stance of curator as master surveyor. What we need to do is to highlight the role of the curator as a collaborator,' I replied.

Stephen then said, 'Sure, let's do it.'

For the next year we wrote funding applications, developed institutional partnerships, and I paired up a dozen artists and writers. No one turned us down. We were swimming in azure waters. The plan was that the artists and writers would correspond with each other before they came together on the 'neutral' ground of the Cornerhouse Gallery and then jointly made their work. My job was to be the funnel and spout of the correspondences. Jimmie and John were the jewels in the crown. No one had produced such marvellous metaphors to evoke the mystery of painting as John, and Jimmie was a genius at turning metaphors into artworks. Suddenly, Stephen got a new job at Southampton City Art Gallery and the new regime at Cornerhouse had no idea of how to pick up the pieces. They promptly returned the money to the funding bodies and ignored my pleas that we should honour the work of the artists and writers.

It was getting dark when I entered the tunnel in the Jura Mountains. On the other side it was raining and there was a massive bridge spanning the gap to the next mountain. Fortunately, there was no wind. Crossing on a bike with an open-face helmet made the magnetic pull of the drop even stronger. Like a tightrope walker my gaze was focused straight ahead.

I pulled up at a café and rang John.

'Stop now and continue in the morning.'

I told him I would keep going. Geneva was within sight. I was on the home stretch. The rain got heavier, but each corner grew in familiarity; the unremarkable chateau at the hilltop of Saint-Jeoire; then the quarry just before the turn for Mieussy; after the short swerve around Ley; and there was Quincy. Dismount.

'Mon Dieu!' shouted John.

Beverly smiled with a cigarette hanging somewhere in darkness between her lips, elbow and bent wrist.

Yves was seventeen by now. He had a little 50cc motorbike and was out with his mates. Heather Rogers was a young artist who had lived in Texas, New Mexico and California. We met at the Glasgow School of Art. She had moved to live with me in Manchester and had arrived in Quincy in advance of me. This was her second visit to Quincy. She had a talent for photography and loved the Spanish artist Juan Muñoz's card tricks. She jumped to my embrace and greeted me with a Mexican nickname.

'Paco!'

On the return leg to the UK on our previous trip, Heather and I presented our passports at the customs office in Dover. We were seated on my BMW Boxer. I had a ponytail and an EU Greek passport. She was a young American woman in leather pants with a valid student visa.

Just as the officer was about to lower the stamp Heather asked if she could get an extension. Heather had beautiful blue eyes, soft brown hair and a voluptuous round face. It was hard to resist her requests. The officer's hand braked just a millimetre before the stamp was due to hit the page and then it screeched into reverse. Her eyes skidded towards Heather's face with suspicion.

Three hours later a group of Polish guys in a rock band came out of the room in which she was detained. One turned to me and said: 'We have been told to turn around. They think we have come here to make money. The American girl is also fucked!'

Heather was that American girl. The custom's investigators had declared that she was at risk of overstaying. They held her passport but granted her the right to go back to Manchester and gather her belongings. She had forty-eight hours, after which she was deported.

John was furious. He rang Anthony Barnett, the founder of Charter 88, a British pressure group that advocated for constitutional reform. That produced some interesting theory. I went to my MP who made it clear that all he would do was to listen for a little while and then, on cue, his secretary stood up as if another meeting beckoned, and they escorted us to the door. Heather got on her plane accompanied by another customs officer. When the seat belt was buckled her passport was returned and the customs officer disembarked.

Heather promptly lost her passport and re-applied for a visa. She returned to Geneva a year later where John and Beverly picked her up.

John encouraged her to be a photographer. She had the lightness of touch that Jean Mohr had mastered. John would handle her photos with tender love and serious admiration. First, he would fumble around for his cheap off-the-shelf lost-and-found glasses. He hated wearing glasses. He cursed his failing eyesight as if they were betraying his masculinity. So he took it out on the glasses whenever they were not sitting in his shirt pocket. Once focus was gained, he would run his fingers along the white edge of the photographs, and then his eyes would dart in: 'You see, you see, the flare and columns of light are just like that, it is there! No one has ever captured the light in the barn the way you have, Heather.'

When I told John of the difficulties we were having to hold together a long-distance relationship, John sent us this poem.

Hay for Heather
Hay is a dry river
          Flowing into a dry lake
flowing uphill for the house dominates
          the fields around and the haybarn
          is under the roof
          massive
          as the hold of a freighter
          in dry dock
Lift when the hay lifts
Shove when she pulls
Hay before man
          is grass clover
          meadowsweet sedge
          columbine cornflower
          common bent
we scythe and weave it into hay
Hay is between river and cloth
Prod behind when it is stubborn
Twist when it is upright
Hay is an animal
who settles in the barn floor
and lets the wind cool it
after mating

Its spray is dust
its stitches sunlight
The forks smile only
When the hay is laying down
For the cows, underfoot
(there are slits in the floor for forking
into their mangers below)
the cloth and the river
are the weather
of winter to come
Climb the ladder
level the torrents
and see with your red eyes
how hay too
can fill a cathedral
like Bach
Its spray is dust
Its stitches sunlight

My father was always punctual. I like to leave a little ahead of time. John is the same. We both hate being late. Heather had an uncanny ability to know how late she could be and still make a flight. I would hide our tickets and lie about the departure time, and somehow, she still adjusted and stretched out her make-up time.

One day John wanted to take us to the market in Samoëns. We were both waiting in the car. Heather said she was coming. We were waiting and still waiting. I was staring out the window. John was switching the engine on and off.

Then John turned to me. Tightened his grip on the steering wheel and, tilting his head back to summon the ancient spirits of Anthony and Cleopatra, he groaned: 'It has been like this since the day of the chariot.'

4. BMW Boxer and Honda Blackbird

I can't say this for certain, but I am pretty sure that John was lousy at sport. He was definitely a goofy dancer and he refused to sing. Musical instruments were held by him in the same awe as astronomers hold for the stars. However, put him in front of any musical instrument, even the basic alphorn, and he froze.

It would often rain during the haymaking season. During these interruptions Yves and I would have epic ping-pong battles. John would put on his BBC commentator's voice as he kept score and revved up his young son. Occasionally he would play the winner. He had a dangerously supple wrist that could unleash a wicked backhand flick smash, but he had no patience to build up a point. On the motorbike he had a light touch and gentle balance. John was a prudent rider. He accepted that riding was risky, but he did not add any unnecessary risks. He loved dressing up in full leathers, gloves and helmet – it was the closest thing to being an astronaut on earth he would say, as he sped off to get fresh bread for the afternoon.

He always rode the latest and fastest Honda. I almost killed myself taking the Blackbird out of the showroom in Annecy. He was stuck in Paris and sent me and Beverly to collect it for him. It had a top speed of 275 km/h and could reach 100 in just over two seconds. My BMW had not changed much since the days of the trenches, his Honda was from the jet age. The Blackbird is a masterpiece. Outside of the showroom Beverly was waiting in her car. She had lit another cigarette. The road was straight. By the time she smiled I had disappeared over the horizon. Yves still rides it.

Speed on the straight valley roads was a thrill for John but his true delight was in gliding along the curving mountain passes. He loved the view from the Col de la Faucille on the Jura Mountains that led to Lac Léman, which Ruskin, with some fairness, described as the best lake in the world. These mountains have a very serious beauty. They don't just stand above you, they are stern, and in a demanding way they seem to look down on you.

What can be more adorable – mountain or sea? I saw the peak of Mont Blanc only once. It was a bright winter's day. Every other day it was veiled by clouds. The surrounding mountains were less reserved. But they all had this evil eye. I always felt rebuked and diminished in their presence. In the summer, as I strolled back to the house after a hard day's work, I felt more assured of my place in the valley. The mountains were always watching. Only the cosmos could humble them. On a clear night the multitude of shining stars made the outline of the mountains shimmer.

The sea, on the other hand, is always in conversation, it whispers, coughs and gushes. It has the energy of a giant lung. Inhale with the waves and exhale onto the sand. Every barefoot step along the tingling foreshore is musical. I am not a fisherman. I learnt to swim without fear late in my life. I still enter dark water with trepidation, but the Mediterranean blue is the most beautiful colour.

John enjoyed swimming. For him it was more like a floating therapy than it was physical exercise.

In a museum John moved like a hunter. He would lean in a bit too close for the comfort of museum guards. On one occasion I was tilting my head to see a painting from the bottom up. He noticed this switch of perspective from a distance, and he came sliding in along the carpet as if he were performing a tackle on a soccer pitch. Leaning on his elbow, he agreed that the view was better from beneath.

During one haymaking season a sequence of storms had descended. It was predicted that there would be a period of at least ten idle days. Heather and I decided to take the overnight train from Geneva to Venice to visit the Biennale. Before we left, John showed me a trick with the index of the guidebook that revealed every church in the lagoon that had a painting by Titian, Tintoretto, Carpaccio or Veronese. He loved Titian. I was drawn to Tintoretto. I still imagine him hunching up and flapping his arms so that the clouds in Renaissance paintings could lift him above the ground.

Somewhere after Milan thieves boarded the train. They gassed the carriage. Forced the lock to our couchette and emptied my wallet that was in my back pocket. I woke up with a slight headache and penniless. I didn't carry a credit card and intended to pay the hotel and our meals like an old cashed-up peasant. We moved into a cheap art hotel, managed to get money from a bank and rationed the gelato and pizzas. In the churches we waited for the American tour groups to arrive and enter coins into the slots that lit up the frescoes and paintings. Heather took photos and I wrote poems inspired by Tintoretto's paintings.

When we returned John ordered a book on Tintoretto. I typed up my poems and printed them from Beverly's computer. John sat with me in the garden and started cutting out reproductions of Tintoretto's painting from the book he purchased. We lay them side by side on large A3 pages. In the evening I read my poems.

San Gerome your beard
echoes the light and curves
of your eyes and nose.
There is your solitude.
...
Amongst all the struggle
between humiliation and repentance
at the foot of your cross shines
an inexhaustible adoration that lightens the flesh pink.
Along the rapturous unburdening of armour

in the moment of conversion
sighs and shrieks
laughter of the blood
and black stooped screams
the city walls stand firm beyond.
Under the leper infected sky
appears
the long stake
bent at the point where the sponge drips with vinegar.
thus
your thirst was dabbed.
...
With the ease of someone that rises from their seat
as the evening bus approaches their stop
tired but already relaxing into the alighting.
With that gentle bending of the knees
and toes pointing down like those majestic moments
that only a few ballerinas can hold for split second infinity.
Then in the straightening of the torso,
as one arm hangs vertically, almost limp
and the other bent at the elbow and pointing up
his face is lit
by a path to the sky.
Home.

John and I had left Heather and Beverly by the side of a lake. We had ridden up on our two bikes. John in the lead.

The French side of Lac Léman was surrounded by dense woods. At the water's edge the soil was soft and almost sandy. People had laid down their towels and were enjoying the strong midday sun. As we walked along the 'beach' I noticed a well-groomed Siberian husky dog, and a middle-aged balding man with a pistol where his pillow should have been, and a young woman in a red bikini. She had just finished a sequence of salutes to the sun and had settled in to read her book – a biography on Freud. Nearby an elegant woman with hair sprayed like Sophia Loren and a leopard-print bikini lay on her towel while her two men caressed her. One was tubby, well-tanned and had shoulder-length hair with blond tips. The other tall, very skinny, and his hair was already grey, but there was a bulbous budgie protruding from his blue briefs.

I said nothing as we approached this odd gathering. John was deep in a discourse on Deleuze. After we got past earshot, I mentioned the pistol.

'Oh, he probably keeps it to protect the dog from thieves. Those dogs are VERY expensive.'

He brushed it off, but I have neither touched a gun, nor done military service. I found it difficult to go back to Deleuze's theory of the fold and Spinoza's ideas on the intertwining of the mind and body. We switched to talking about the lean perch and carp that, unlike the farmed trout and salmon, had to swim against the currents deep in the alpine lakes. We picked some flowers. I could only distinguish the flowers by colour and shape. John could see names and functions. The tall purple ones were bellflowers. The paler and drooping vetch was good for spider bites. The peony also is very common. Aristotle and his student Theophrastus were very sceptical of folk wisdom – they dismissed much of it as far-fetched and irrelevant. For instance, Theophrastus noted that many believed that the peony 'should be dug up at night, for if a man does it in the daytime and is watched by a woodpecker while he gathers fruit, he risks the loss of his eyesight. If he is cutting the root at the time, then he will suffer a prolapsed anus.' Louis would chuckle at such stories, he knew that they were 'poetic', worth telling to pass the time and fill in the gaps, but that did not mean he believed them. We cut our peonies and our eyes and anus remained fine. With a beautiful bunch of sunny dandelions, red compagnon and yellow herb bennett in hand we ambled back to the women.

The man with the pistol and the silky husky were gone, the young woman was deep in her Freud, the men were quarrelling over who should apply oil on the lady's back.

Beverly unzipped a tiny smile at the gift of flowers. We decided to pick up the blanket, load up the Kaiser panniers on the Boxer and head back home. We swapped passengers and Beverly snuggled in behind me. John pulled out of the gravel parking area, but then gave the signal for me to lead. On the days that there was no haymaking he found it hard to relax, he was restless and worried about the possibility of the rain ruining the harvest.

Riding a motorbike in Europe you never feel alone. As I cruised into small towns, I could sense that people would be bemused by my German bike, British plates and Aussie stickers. Every time a rider overtakes another rider they release a gesture of solidarity – a downward-flick wave of the hand, or a little up-kick with the foot. If you stop on the side of the road, the next rider will check to see if you need assistance.

Beverly was the best pillion. My old friend Scott McQuire was like a parachute. Heather a blinking lighthouse – always scanning left and right. Beverly did not reach back for the grips on the back of the seat. She used her knees and thighs for balance, scooped her lower back down, leaned lightly into my shoulders and gently held onto my belt. She breathed with supreme trust in me and the bike. Submitted to every corner like a supple stalk of grass blown by a gentle wind. I could barely notice her. No flapping resistance, and no clapping of our helmets during braking.

Coming down the mountain we were mostly in the shade and with an open-face helmet you could smell the moist moss. Between the Arolla pine trees there were lateral glimpses of the valley below and above us the rock face. My bike felt clean and smooth. My head was empty. The road on this mountain was cut with sympathy – it collaborated with the contours. The descent was a divine exercise in counter-steering. On the Boxer, with its flat handlebars, this is easy. Before he got the Blackbird, John had a Honda CBR1000F. The handles on this bike incline towards the pilot and they are so sensitive you must probe like a dentist. With countersteering, a slight nudge of your wrist on the handlebar and the wheel turns in the opposite direction to where you want to go. This causes the bike to lean the other way, and if your body is in sync with the machine and you let go of the need to follow logic, then you will glide around the corner. As the road straightens you apply another nudge on the other handlebar. A gentle lunge as you go up a gear. Soft hands and keeping your body low with the fairing really helps.

Geometry and not Formula One acrobatics does the work. The road has a painted dividing line, but as a pilot your mind is on an invisible line that cuts each section of the lane into straight segments. In a car, driving through the perspective of a window frame, you never see this line. The pilot on a bike, unlike the driver, is not just looking ahead, he must always scan for cars that might jump an intersection, or search for the potholes below. Along the verge I saw a rabbit popping up above the grass field, but so did the kestrel which swooped past my visor and picked up dinner.

I was in the zone and John was in my slipstream. John was normally a commanding rider. He loved to ride on his own. However, he relished the bond that was formed down this descent.

Getting off a bike is always a mood change, like the end of a deep tissue Thai massage. John was elated. He also liked to follow.

I am a terrible procrastinator. I am also hopeless at storing photographs. Writing this book has released me from the academic quest to find an exact order for things. It has let me drop into the zone of an amber light – pausing, reflecting, slowing down, and holding.

Quincy is at an elevation of 800 metres. However, even in the short distance between and John's and Louis's houses the road starts a steep incline. Above the village there is a ridge – Pointe de Marcelly which stands at 2000 metres. From that point paragliders would launch themselves on some glorious summer mornings. They would skim the crisp mountain air and sweep the valley until they landed in the sports fields of Mieussy. Paragliding, or *parapente*, was invented here in 1978.

Every year I looked up in wonder at the luminous triangular wings that glistened silently in the sky. I would say to myself, next year I will do this. Beverly would smile encouragingly. John grimaced, scrunched up his eyes, and looked the other way. He had an incurable fear of flying. He once went to Russia, but that was by boat. He said he refused to go to America on political grounds. His regular trips to Sweden were always on the Honda. The short flight to a remote Scottish island, and the trip to visit his pregnant daughter in Athens took all his courage, a huge breath and heavy dose of tranquillisers before take-off. He eventually did go to New York. It only confirmed his disgust.

'Never again!' he said.

I can't imagine that his fear was linked to the rush that comes from the first thrust of the plane's engine. Surely that was a buzz akin to a great gear change. My friend Janis Jefferies once shared a flight with me from London to Granada. Her hands were tiny. As we sat, she asked if she could hold my hand. Her fear was confined to the moment of take-off. When the plane moved, her hand clasped on top of mine and closed like a steel vice. She turned as white as a marble statue and shut her eyes as if a monster were approaching. When the plane levelled, she let go of my hands, and her skin thawed. Maybe John needed the hand of strangers. Or maybe, he just sat there still as a hunter – looking for signs of danger in the frowns of the stewards and listening for any hint of gurgling in the engines.

One of the older women in the village shared my wish to glide from the high rock to the bottom of the valley.

She always dressed in black. Her children had emigrated to the city. One day she approached the three men who still ran the *parapente* school and persuaded one of them to take her for a ride. They explained how she could piggyback with them, and the following week, she flew across the village.

John could not believe his eyes. There was the woman in black framed by a sail striped in yellow, green and purple. They made multiple spiralling circles, and he could hear her laughter. Odile, the narrator of the story *Once in Europa*, tells her life story in the valley from the perspective of the passenger on a *parapente*.

The narrator for *Lilac and Flag* was also born in this wish to escape from gravity. John told me that the story could not find its spark until he found an aerial viewpoint for his narrator. The genesis of 'The Three Lives of Lucie Cabrol' had a similarly fraught beginning. John could not commence until he found a specific perspective from which he could tell the story. In this case, the migrant eye was found in the man who once loved her.

'In real life there was such a woman called Lucie Cabrol who was in fact murdered like I tell it in my story. Again, this story that I tried to write on many occasions but couldn't until I realised that the story should be told by a man who had once loved her when she was young. As soon as I found or invented that man who had emigrated to Argentina and come back, then I could write that story. The voice came.'

John's trilogy of peasant life is filled with characters that were both a product of his imagination and were from nearby. They were not direct portraits, but their presence was overflowing in him. I could sense this abundance. I felt the same towards him. At times he overwhelmed me. Not in any overt and imposing manner, but the constant stream of inquisitiveness was hard to match. To write about a beloved friend requires a willingness to float up with their gusts and currents. However, for me, it also required a long arc of time and a release from my own sense of paternal duty.

'We have entered the land of Bruegel,' chuckled John.

The goose was loose, the lame goat was tied to a post, lambs suckled, and cows wandered freely. A short man with a big belly, pork pie hat and not so many teeth, stopped, stared at us for a bit and then smiled.

To enter the village, we had to pass under an archway. It was not quite as fussy and brutal in its arrogance as the Zytglogge in Berne, but it made its own triumphant announcement: Here ends both the asphalt and the French Republique. The earthen track was pounded. The grass was ruffled and untaxed.

John had been complaining of a sore back.

His friend Anthony Barnett, who had been his editor at *New Society* in the 1960s and 1970s, told me, when we met in 2016 at the launch of the Democracy in Europe Movement (DiEM) in Berlin, that John had always moaned about his back.

Yet a man with a sore back, imaginary or real, is not much use in the barn. Yves asked around the villages. His friend Loic, whose family were builders of log cabins and often suffered from sciatica, suggested a *guérisseuse* – a healer – in a remote village on the far side of the mountains.

None of us knew the way. Yves was pillion with John. I was following on the Boxer. I could see Yves's arms waving – left, right, turn around, straight.

The man with the pork pie hat pointed out the house of the *sseuse*. We entered through the kitchen. It looked rather ordinary. A checked red tablecloth, chairs with cane weaving, maybe one or two too many icons of the Madonna, but nothing really freaky.

Then she entered the room with total command. She was plump with short grey hair and thick glasses. She was dressed in woollen clothes that in the Alps are suitable for all seasons. Her voice was stern, but there was a slight smile at the edge of her mouth.

John was told to lift his shirt and bend over the table. Yves and I were instructed to leave. As we were leaving, we could hear her breathing heavily and chanting up and down his back.

Yves and I walked past the tethered goat and noticed that a barn with a wagon wheel nailed to the door carried a faded sign saying *café*. There were also some bottles of soft drink with labels that neither of us recognised. We helped ourselves.

Yves raised his bottle. 'Here's to you, bastard!'

He hummed a few bars of: 'Yum-yum, Yum de dum, Here they come, Yum-yum, Yum de dum, Here come the bastards.'

We left some money on the barrels that served as stools and strolled back to the bikes, wondering whether the *sseuse* was still mixing up a poultice with resin and herbs.

John appeared soon after. He looked a bit groggy but claimed that whatever it was it helped. He felt something lift.

We got back on the bikes and exited under the arch. Heading back John took us via the road that skirts Lac Léman and then turned into the former sanatorium that is now a famous restaurant frequented by rich widows.

John did all the shopping. In Quincy the café had closed and there is no store. However, there is a market on different days of the week in the neighbouring towns of Mieussy, Taninges, Morzine and Samoëns.

The brimming cornucopia of regional produce is for John like the silk lining to the day's jacket. Going to market is not a disruption. He would leave home with purpose but once there he is already sated and light. In the market the need for provisions is suspended in the net of pleasant smiles. The art of making deals is performed with guttural delight.

In the market I am immediately distracted by the van with soft cheeses. John is trying not to look. A disc-shaped camembert dusted with ash is winking at us. John steps in. He is looking deeper at the white rind. The young girl in a white smock and round face greets him. No one would confuse him for a peasant or a factory worker. In this market he is not known as an author. She offers to help.

John hesitates. Vacillating between leaning over the glass and backing out. His loyalty is to Louis's hard cheese. But then he gushes.

'Okay. Okay. Hmmm. Oui. Oui. I will take this little wheel.'

He is still struggling to admit his temptation. I give him a conspiratorial smile and my eyes promise to say nothing. He tucks the little package into the bag, and I extend my hand to carry it. Opposite, the Vietnamese store holder has a new vegetable on sale. Eureka! This would go well with fish. He chats and then buys twice as much as is necessary. The woman plunges the leaves into a plastic bag and John's upper lip rises to meet the bottom of his nose. His lip is expressing anticipation and gratitude as his head is nodding.

'We are not in a supermarket.' He sighs. Not even the light rain will force us to hurry.

'Let's go over to the fishmonger.'

His caravan has fish on beds of crushed ice. The man who is serving is tall. His hands bulge out of his closed elasticated sleeves and his wedding ring is almost hidden by his plump pink flesh. John has seen a long fish. They are discussing the depth of the lake from which it has come and the customs taxes. I am staring at its purple eyes.

I am thinking to myself John wants to draw this fish. He is noticing the gradation from the white belly to the speckled olive green on the gills, the touch of turquoise on the tail, and the black spine. He will use charcoal and pastels. They are blaming the government for everything. John spins his index finger in the air. The fishmonger wraps it in newspaper.

John never shops for more than a single meal at a time. I would hoard things. My greedy eyes rove across the caravan with the hanging salamis and the rows of duck pâté. I could eat here forever. I feel guilty as salt. John jolts me. I have found a small jar with goat's cheese floating in olive oil and garnished with rosemary. I buy it and promise to sprinkle it over the salad. He welcomes this as a piece of my origin being received on the table. I also remind him that we must pass by the baker on the way home.

We hop back into the red Renault. Beverly would use this car for her chores and trips to the airport. John sees me admiring an old Citroën 2CV.

'That is a classic. When was it made?' I ask.

'Soon after the Second World War. They were meant to be a French equivalent to the German Volkswagen. They were designed for country people. An "umbrella with wheels" but big enough to carry the family. The back would flip up so that you could transport the sacks of potatoes to the market.'

I think to myself, if I ever buy a car, it will be a Citroën.

5. Memory Jealousy Eros

Midway through writing this book I had a dream.

Earlier on in the day, I had rinsed my daughter's clothes that had been soaking in a green bucket.

In my dream, I was pouring detergent into the black metal bucket that I normally use for recycling wastepaper. The proportion of water to liquid soap was inverted. The detergent was brimming. Catching myself I tried to return the detergent into the bottle, which had become a porrón – a Spanish decanter with both a wide opening and a narrow spout from which wine spurts. With a slight lift the wine arcs across the gap between your arm and mouth. You can drink from it without your lips touching, and it can be passed to a friend in mid flow. As I poured the detergent down the wider hole it rushed up the narrow one. To prevent it from spilling I tried to catch the liquid in the same black bucket that I was pouring from. The dreamer in me thought that this was impossible.

Then the dream woke me up.

Who or what governs the path of memory? For good and for bad it takes wrong turns, jumps obstacles and bonds foreign things. At times memory seems to be making its own way, refusing to be subject to rhyme or reason.

Last night my friend Don, who is ninety-two, stopped midway in our conversation: 'I am trying to think of what I was just thinking about.'

His grip on memory is slippery. John was lucid until the end. Don was my first mentor. He was born in 1930. The same year as Teodor and my father. Writing this memoir has returned me to stories I have told my friends again and again, but it has also turned up so many unexpected connections. Finding these lost thoughts is like discovering an unexpected current running through my body.

My ancestors and John's neighbours lived a similar life. There is an uneasy symmetry between his journey from the London art world to the French village, and my parents leaving their Greek village in Macedonia as peasants to become 'wogs that turned the cogs' in the factories of Melbourne.

How to bring forth a history that silenced the voice of the peasants? These peasants lived without records. Their stories are in the rhythm of their dances, the patterns in their woven rugs and the structures of their houses.

The pungent odour of the stable is unforgettable. As is the sweet smell of your own perspiration when it is mixed up with the warm heat of fresh hay settling in the loft. In that space, of the mind and the stable, the light enters like laser beams. Can memory bring everything back?

Yves is still there in the village. In my mind I see him in the loft. He is still a teenager in his sweat-stained t-shirt and the light-blue baseball cap worn in reverse. His hair is short and golden brown. The dust has left a dark ring along the top of his forehead.

'Papa, we're almost done!'

I try to connect the seasonal cycle in Quincy with rhythms of my suburban garden in Melbourne. First the white of jasmine announces the arrival of spring, the gardenia follows with its supreme scent, and finally, the ebullient red bougainvillea claims its summer triumphs along my fence.

I have the urge to read aloud the pages from this book. I am convinced that if I start reading John will appear across the table. First, he squints. His mouth and chin fold in together. Then, he will clasp his fingers, lean in, and the day will crown when I hear him laugh.

As he got older John's metabolism slowed down. Although he ate no more than the rest of us, and worked just as hard if not harder, his belly started to bulge. His gestures were still full of fizz. His leonine features never left him, and his light-blue eyes made his gaze both delicate and intense.

He was proud to call himself a storyteller. Somehow this title covers all the bases – poet, revolutionary, philosopher, artist, writer, moralist. It gave him the licence to explore his instincts and reflect on the experience of others. It allowed him to conjure fabulous associations but also cogitate about the point of it all. He could not bear the thought of writing about himself as if he were some discrete and precious little island, but then again, almost all his protagonists had a variation on the name John – Janos, Giovanni, Juan, Jean.

Listening to other people recall their dreams is utterly boring. I felt such pity for a friend who described the ritual at the Sunday breakfast table as his girlfriend's father paraded his previous night's dream.

In John's house I slept well. My recurring nightmares of house invaders were left behind in Manchester. However, on more than one occasion I woke up screaming – a jealous rage had left me covered in sweat.

The theatre director and actor Simon McBurney also came to help one year. He arrived with his new script for a play. In the afternoons Simon and John would sit at the little white table in the garden. Simon would ask a series of practical questions.

'Should she sing or read the line?'

'Should she be wearing green or black?'

John would tug on his chin, roll back his head to imagine the scenario and go up into the atmosphere as if he were solving an equation in quantum physics, and then suddenly, as he returned, all four legs of the chair would sink a little deeper in the grass: 'Yes! Yes! Sing! Green!'

I am not sure Simon was cut out for the country life. His ancestors were all surgeons and scholars. The heat and dust got to him. During our breaks he had to strip naked, and totally dunk himself in the cow's trough to cool off. He had fine brown hair. When he shook himself dry his hair would rise in a spiky crown.

Sharing John with Simon was annoying. I don't know how Yves put up with us.

In my dream I put a firewall around John. The sinister side of my love was that it wanted to close the door. Block him from fleeing. Only his family and village friends were to be allowed sanctuary. I wanted to hold him in as if that place were the whole of the world. Nothing else needed to pass. Even time could rest in this enclosed garden. The trees could offer shade, we would have coffee in the morning, the day's chores all done, everything would be perfect, and I would smile like an emperor. No one else would notice. I would be greedy, but everything would be normal. My unchecked love assumed it could blur care with control. It entered without knocking and assumed that the bed was always free. This home was taken without asking. The host and guest had been merged in my dreaming mind.

But who was it that I really wanted to keep out? Rivals, which rivals? Not painters. Some came and went. They wanted small things. His approval and maybe a few words for their catalogue. The great artists began their relationship with John through correspondence. They opened the big windows of conversation and let in other worlds. Such artists were always welcome, because in my mind they were neither going to stay, nor threatening to take John away.

The ones I felt jealous of were the artists that both came and then transported John to their imaginary garden. When they came, I felt null and void. We could all be in the kitchen, talking and preparing dinner, but the artist and John were in a bubble. Even when the food was on the table, John would take another drag on his cigarette. Dinner was going cold. No one else was visible. In the competition, I would be the sulking fiend. Rather than putting another idea on the table I would simmer resentfully, silently, and in my other mind sarcastically dismiss the other's project as a waste of time.

Even in the dream of jealous rage I had no words to put in the middle of this desolation. I preferred silent indignation because I had already accepted that my voice could not compete. I was reduced to silence because the only words were ones that came from inside my insecurity. It needed another voice. But in its absence, I could only scream. Was this shriek aimed to awaken John, to bring him to his senses, and force this other artist to leave immediately?

In the morning, he is still there, drinking coffee while sitting in my spot.

I become even more tyrannical. Slicing every gesture with my evil eye, counting time, checking for signs of exit, and wondering if my imagined peace of the garden will ever be restored.

All day I would be covered in a film of the bitter sweat of guilt. Stuck in my head, thinking of ways to recycle wine, to pour back memories that have overspilled.

Then another voice would enter my head.

How dare I pretend to be emperor! In what world could my love be sufficient to sustain everything! How lazy! I wanted to control the gate, but I was just a passive guard that wanted to keep everything. John was always the active lover not the passive beloved. He would refuse even the most gilded lover's cage. Being watched was not his style. To keep him in this state would be another way of cutting off his oxygen. John loved it when visitors arrived with a vehicle. He loved the prospect of turning a rough idea inside out. He pursued precision, strove to debunk illusions, played with form – not for power – but in the hope of gaining the love that comes with truth and justice. Money and rewards only mattered as a means to keep going. Recalling such jealous memories makes me shrivel and shrink.

The sovereign dream was a compensation for my own lack of

preparedness and imagination. I had the pathetic expectation that arriving on my bike loaded with a few gifts was all that we needed. I did not come with a plan, or an agenda, let alone a project into which John could be implicated. Not even a few questions. Just the assumption that, once here, all would be found. I wanted my arrival to be received with expectation, unfold into an organic collaboration, and then yield a luminous achievement. I had the fantasy that once there, everything else would grow by itself.

Jealousy is a grotesque urge that kills every impulse for hospitality and floods the body with bile. How ugly it must have looked, and I now dread the thought that John saw all of this. Looking back into the kitchen I see both Jealous Nikos and another Nikos that neither condemns nor loves. This other Nikos is there and not there. He goes to the cellar to replenish the empty bottles of wine, and everyone else keeps drinking.

My father suffered from Parkinson's disease. It is a miserable and humiliating diminishment of a man. My mother struggled to care for him but also resolutely refused to admit him into a nursing home. The cognitive errors compounded, and the risks increased. He put the electric kettle on the gas stove flame and walked away waiting for the whistle to blow. The fire alarm went off instead.

The second time this happened I sat with him on a couch in the kitchen.

'What if next time you were alone with your granddaughter, and she died in the fire, but you walked out into the garden and survived?'

He cried. When I asked again if he would go to a nursing home, he offered no resistance. In fact, he expressed relief. My mother's pride was still an obstacle. She only relented when she found a spot in the nursing home that she frequented as a volunteer.

That nursing home was a stone's throw from the first house we lived in, in South Melbourne. Every night we would go to bed with the tolling of the town hall bells. My godfather's house was visible from the window of my father's new room. Despite the familiarities, the adjustment was awful. My father would have delirious outbursts. He screamed and yelled. He was convinced that cow thieves were lurking, and, when he calmed down, he felt obliged to drive home the nurses. He was once again both a *tsobano* – a shepherd/berger – in Greece and a taxi driver in Australia.

After he settled, I told him that my daughter Maya, my wife Victoria Lynn and I were going to the Greek island of Kefalonia for our summer vacation. It was on this island that he had completed his military service. He had been stationed there after the catastrophic earthquake in 1953. It struck with a magnitude of 7.2 on the Richter scale. This was equivalent to the detonation of four H-bombs exploding under the island. The rupture was so powerful that the island lifted upwards by about sixty centimetres. Almost all the buildings were flattened and 450 people lost their lives. Kefalonia is poised at the intersection of the African and European plates. Sailors and soldiers came to the rescue of the stunned survivors. My father helped clear the rubble and he often recounted that he had carved his name on a tree near a ruined school. When he heard me say 'Kefalonia' his eyes lifted towards the white ceiling.

'Divarata, Patrikata, Drapanitika, Konidarata, Makoulata, Touliata, Bentoniata, Antipata, Germenata.'

He was frothing slightly at the mouth. I did not recognise these names. I thought he was lapsing into another delirious rant. Ata, ata, ata, ata – these are not Greek name endings. Antonin Artaud's final mad outbursts were not in French but in his native Greek that he spoke with his nannies in Smyrna. In his final delirium he called out for nani nanaki and his old Antonaki.

When we flew into Kefalonia we realised that the pension was at the other end of the island. We drove along the road that follows the spine of the mountain. Dodging the goats that were sleeping amongst the rocks that slipped off the ridges we wove our way past the villages. The moon was splendid, and the village signs were actually legible. The legacy of Venetian names came alive. All the names ended in 'ata'. Midway I realised that my father's rant was a precise recollection of all the names that run from one end of the island to the other.

In his final days, the words totally dissipated. There were tiny crystal moments of humour, but then long silences. A rigid passivity chilled the room.

The day before he died, I had a massive nosebleed. I could not stop it and paramedics were called to my office at the university. After they managed to stop it and cleaned me up, I decided to visit Dad. As I entered his nursing home I saw Tony Tiganis, my best friend during high school. My body instantly relaxed. We went upstairs and sat next to my father's bed.

Dad had not eaten for over a fortnight. He was now as stiff as a plank, but his formidable heart kept its regular beat. His breathing was gentle, but he no longer squeezed my finger when I put it in his hand.

Is there life without memory? How much, or what kind of memory is enough to make a life worth living? Is it the thread that you keep, to hang in there? I once thought that this bare existence was not living. If I were in such a predicament, I would rather end it.

I often found my father in the common room of the nursing home. He would be staring at the surface of the matt lemon formica table. I would greet him, and he would not budge. But when Maya approached, I saw a flash of the old twinkle in my father's eyes. This brief glimpse of joy made me wonder what other pleasure lingered beneath. It forced me to doubt my own judgement of how much one needs to fill a day. Is it enough that he saw Maya? Did the bottle refill itself?

Tony and I chatted for hours. My brother Vasili dropped by and seeing that everything seemed calm he went home to his kids. Tony was giggling as he recalled our teenage pranks. He recounted the time my father walked into my room just after we smoked a joint. Dad was carrying a tray of cookies and could smell the dope from the kitchen. He smiled as he asked Tony why his eyes were blood shot, and Tony pulled out the pouch of tobacco and said, 'I think this is too strong Johnny.' My father pretended to agree and left us to our bullshit.

It is terrifying to try to grasp the dimensions of the mind when it oscillates between short blips of lucid connection and the abyss of amnesiac resignation. What was happening to my father when I spoke to him? Was this sweet but faraway silence like being stoned?

Tony and I stayed late into the night. I felt a sort of contentment that my father was listening to our babbling conversation. I was sure that he was grinning with complicity at the sound of Tony's provocations. I went home, had supper and went to bed.

Shortly after midnight I received the last call from the nursing home. My brother and I returned to witness giant-sized morticians as they zipped up the wine-red body bag. The town hall bells did not toll. The night nurse was new. Amber lights punctuated the night. I drove home along Albert Park Lake. He always liked the soft asphalt and hourglass curve of that road.

I don't want to die because I don't want the memories I hold of all the people I love to disappear. At least I don't want to die until my daughter Maya can hold some of these lives in her body. For almost three millennia Greeks have prided themselves for possessing a culture of the book. However, all my ancestors worked the fields of stone and mud. I was lucky to be the first to live by writing. I have neither lived in their villages, nor can I write into their silences. My struggle is not to find immortality, but it is against capricious history. Our peasant history almost evaporated. Costa-Gavras, the Greek filmmaker based in Paris, came from a humble background. His mother was a peasant, and she was very religious. My parents only went to church at Easter and for special events like a wedding. They never mentioned the priests in their village. Costa-Gavras's mother took him to church every Sunday. He sat there oblivious to the meaning of the two-and-a-half-hours-long ceremony. He loved justice, but he also loved his mother. While his films attacked the state and capitalism, he never exposed the hypocrisy of the church. He was from where he was from. His films could not bridge all these worlds.

Luis Buñuel claimed that in his childhood village of Calanda 'the Middle Ages lasted until World War I'. (Buñuel: 10) The cataclysmic changes of modernity – colonisation, migration and industrialisation – the ruptures of peasant life and the dismantling of feudal power – were somehow delayed in his part of Aragon. The first years of his life were dominated by the rituals of church life and the comforts brought by his father's entrepreneurial gains in Cuba. Buñuel played but did not work with the children of the peasants. He recalled the names of the aristocrats but not the servants. Chores were done in his village in more or less the same way as they were done in Roman days. The weather was still and dry. Progress wafted by like the clouds, but to him it did not touch his village. Buñuel only encountered the modern world when the family moved to Zaragoza and then to Madrid. His lifelong inclinations and dispositions – the ironic detachment and acerbic curiosity, the persistent drum rhythms and ongoing flirtation with violence, the passive resignation to cosmic cycles and satisfaction with simple fried eggs and chorizo – were all linked back to Calanda and its deep peasant history. These elements were there in his films but the bridges between them were few.

The stone steps leading to the church in my father's village Skalohori were well worn and made shiny by generations of feet.

Thousands of wooden clogs and pigskin *tsarouchia* had pressed on them. In John's village the clogs were called *sabots*. Walking along the path represented a transition. Away from the stables and up to the higher ground of the church. The working mind and body would go on pause. It was a ceasefire from the day. But the sound of *tsarouchia* also amplified the sound of grumbling tummies in the winter and was a counterpoint to the squeal of the pig as it was slaughtered in the spring. Time spun in the crook of the village's arm.

My father enjoyed putting on his suit and tie for church services in Australia. 'Not every day is the same.'

Dressing up for festivities was a way of marking time and making the ancestors feel proud.

Time twirled and space warped. The village was small, and everyone knew everything. If something needed to be done, the path for its completion was familiar. At night the shepherds would rest on the hilltop above the village, and dream of elsewhere. Maybe the world was just another village, magnified but not different. By then shepherds like my father had heard stories of men who had been to the city. They had returned with stories full of secrets. In whispers, they revealed guilty pleasures, unimaginable colours, and bragged about spectacular deals. Am I now recycling the memory of my father through the story of *A Seventh Man*? How did history deplete us so?

John and my father had the same bitter-sweet body odour.

My father came home with a second-hand Holden station wagon. It was in two-tone grey and had protruding wings for the rear lights. In the summer we would pack for picnics. My cousins and I would sit on the esky – drinks cooler – in the back. Waving and making funny faces at all the drivers and passing passengers. When I sat on the front bench seat between my mother and my father I could breathe in his scent. His arms above my head holding the wheel.

John loved to wear cologne. Even if he wasn't going anywhere, he liked to put on Kouros Aftershave. When we sat in the shade, waiting for Louis to arrive with the next load, he often wiped his brow, and as he sat up with his back against the barn wall, he rested his elbow on his knee. As I lay flat beside him, his scent descended. It was almost the same as the aroma in my father's car.

As a child I remember my father's sense of care and pride in his family. It tended to come out in goofy ways. Insisting that we all dance as soon as the music started. Never saying no when I pointed to a toy at the stalls in the South Melbourne market. Always deferring to the authority of my mother, even when he gave me that conspiratorial look, that suggested conceding to her was right even if she was wrong. I remember my father through the outline of his face and body. He was fast and strong. But that strength carried millennia of peasant endurance and three decades of factory subservience.

At the end of my first year as a tutor in political science at the University of Melbourne I began editing journals. I became involved with a collective called *Arena* that owned its own antiquated lead set printing press. I was enchanted by the whole production process. My father had worked in a printing press as a guillotine operator. He could line up the paper with precision. The manager was fond of his positive attitude and would let me hang around on school holidays. The machine was huge, and my father had all the English skills that it required. When the arms and blades were set at the right angles, he only needed two words: Stop, Go. To make it even easier they were in red and green.

When I brought home the first copy of a journal with my name printed in the contents page, he was sitting in the kitchen playing backgammon with my uncle.

'Look baba, it has my name on it.'

He looked up. Put down his dice. Picked up the journal. Turned to examine the glue on the spine and flicked through the pages. His eyes darted like a hawk on a rabbit.

'The lines are not straight.'

He rolled the dice and continued the game of trying to trap my uncle in the corner of the board. I walked into the living room and chatted with my mother and aunt. They were talking about how much freedom kids should have. That was more interesting than the destiny cast by dice.

I don't remember spending much time looking into my father's eyes. I looked elsewhere for recognition and rebellion. I would talk to him in abstract hypotheticals and only when thoughts had been resolved. He did little to block me and felt that the highest duty on earth was to sacrifice himself on the altar of his children's education.

When I first met John, I fell into his eyes. The more we talked the more intense the gaze.

Where was this look in my father's eyes? It seemed buried under the calluses in the hands that cupped his face. Twice he cried. Once when his mother died. The other when he crashed his taxi without the cover of insurance. On both occasions he hid his face in hands. I was a teenager, content to be alone but also confused with the fear of drifting in a fatherless world.

6. What Does the Bachelor Peasant Dream?

Louis Sauge sits on his tractor. Scratches his stubble. Lifts his flat cap to freshen the air. He stares at the clouds and observes the wind in the trees. To narrow down the scope of vision he concentrates on a small section of sky. He reaches into his pocket. There is no wallet or keys, just a handkerchief. He wipes his brow. The mountains have already compressed the horizon. It is this abundance of peaks that makes the shifts in the weather more volatile. A nervous twitch comes through his eyes.

Can he see the flowers on the verge?

Does he still hear the chirping of the birds?

The tractor is in idle. He is grumbling. Is it going to rain now or later? The air is cooling. His fingers are tapping out a beat on the steering wheel. His nose is alert to the intoxicating smell of cut grass. Louis stands up from his seat. His shoulders relax but his head is full of calculations. When speaking of politics, he makes generalisations seem like light work. However, this weather forecast business bothers him. Getting it wrong is not a life-or-death matter, but it causes waste. *That* annoys him!

Life is simple and hard.

It is even harder keeping it simple.

His eyes dart up to the clouds over the mountains. They are getting thicker. The black outlines overshadowing the grey and white. They are running north to south. Their speed is increasing. He curses the weatherman who predicted a dry day. He has already cut one field and dreads the loss of nutrients as the rain causes rot. It will rain, he concludes, as he glares at his mountains.

He is neither happy nor unhappy.

Louis owned three houses, several fields that were full of nitrogen-rich alfalfa grass and seventeen cows. From the end of his street, on a rare fine day, there was the magnificent view of Mont Blanc. At 4800 metres it is the pinnacle of Europe. On my first visit I saw it, promptly took it for granted, but never saw the peak again. It was almost always cloud-covered. When Louis's house was built the region was back in the hands of the Duke of Savoy. For a brief period, Haute-Savoie was annexed by the French revolutionaries, and they renamed the region as the department of Mont Blanc. It was only at the end of the nineteenth century that it formally became part of France.

The cows, of course, had to be milked every single day. By the afternoon their udders were full, and they lowed. In the spring, John would say that the grass 'grows before your eyes'. The cows would get frisky as they smelt it from the barn. In the summer, they would totter up the fields and enjoy the lush mountain grass. Every morning and evening Louis would deposit two churns of milk at the local dairy. This region is the home to some of the best cheesemakers in the world.

In the winter the cows stayed in the barn and were fed hay, and some grains that John mischievously called Mars Bars. Louis called out to his cows with fondness. Each cow had a cute name, like Chloe or Clementine. The kind of name a grandfather would choose if he was permitted to name his daughter's child. As they came down the mountain side, they followed a muddy path. Their hooves cut into the soft damp earth. Swaying and rocking, their bells tinkled and together they formed a languid chorus. A long line of large elm trees shaded the journey all the way down to the stables.

These cows can stare. But what do they see in me that deserves such longing attention? When they catch your eyes their head tilts ever so slightly to one side and then slowly sways to the other. When they are in the field it feels as if they are focusing both on the outline of my head and the mountains in the distance. Do they see something else in between and further into the distance? I stare back hoping to find there the countenance of my ancestors.

Apart from his year of military service Louis never left his cows. He never saw the Mediterranean Sea or the Atlantic Ocean. In his lifetime the village shrunk. All the young women had left to get jobs in factories. In exchange for the mud and shit, they got to work in factories making tiny parts for the aeronautical industry and for four weeks of annual holiday.

Louis was pensive and courteous, but he also had a devilish glance. He loved to add some drops of *gnole* (his moonshine) on sugar cubes and then suck on them. Sugar was rare and expensive in Louis's youth. It arrived in slabs, and it was carefully cut into blocks. Now Louis buys cubed sugar in a packet with a perforated lid. He keeps it at the table. Most of his back teeth are missing.

If I brought a girlfriend to the village, he would start the morning with an expression that mixed self-mockery and vicarious delight: '*Dormir cava, Nikos*!'

These greetings, relative to his overall demeanour, were quite effusive. He was generally polite but also a little withdrawn. If you came over while he was trying to fix a broken part in a machine, he could be agitated. I was told that, like most in the village, he distrusted dealers, and when he was buying or selling, he would use silence as a defensive weapon. He kept his wallet in the drawer of the kitchen sideboard. Money rarely changed hands. It was mostly static not liquid. The car keys were left in the ignition. At night he liked to make an omelette with mushrooms.

When Yves and his mates were around eighteen years old they took me to a local dance in Mieussy. The hall was rectangular and well lit. The big band on the stage had been replaced by a DJ on the floor. A mirrorball spun as twenty couples danced in the middle. The tables with white clothes and half-empty glasses were near the entrance.

In Louis's youth this was the venue where the young would meet.

It was a place of awkward encounters. Men would arrive in small groups. Lean along the side wall and keep their hands in their pockets. They wanted to stare towards the middle of the room, but mostly their eyes were down at their feet and clinging onto each other for some little signs of confirmation. The slightly older men, who had decided that dancing was for the young and the foolish, stayed at the bar. With their shoulders hunched up, they talked about things that they could discuss anywhere. They would speak derisively about women. The men outnumbered the women three to one. When the married ones returned to their tables their wives would scold them for talking to blockheads who think playing cards until dawn is a feast.

On this night Louis was dancing a waltz. Without any envy towards the husbands, whose wives had agreed to dance, Louis moved tenderly and precisely. I could barely recognise his poise and rhythm. He moved slowly around the barn. He had a languid gait. Peasants walked as if they were dragging a heavy scythe behind them. Their legs bowed and feet stuck in the earth. In the dance hall he was light on his toes. His knees were relaxed and his hips fluid. When he raised his arms to spin his partner, she slipped effortlessly into the turn. His eyes were bright and sharp. There was no heavy look of expectation. All week he wore crusty boots with long laces tied around his ankles. At the dance he wore low-cut black shoes. His feet were in a foreign land, but it was a holiday.

After the waltz was over, he walked his dancing partner back to her table. He spotted me and stopped in the middle of the hall. He had the glow of a light sweat. The music was still in his chest. He was happy to see me.

'Nikos, you don't recognise me with teeth!'

He was wearing a light-blue short-sleeved shirt and grey pleated trousers that were crisply pressed. His hair was combed, his moustache clipped, and his face was clean-shaven. And he had gleaming dentures. I did not know the women he was dancing with. I had not seen any of these people before. They must have come from the nearby factories and shops. The women were in bright floral dresses, and their husbands in Lacoste shirts. They were not from the farms. Louis seemed comfortable in the hall. The women who danced with him did not accept his invitation out of pity, or in the expectation of a return of favour. They knew he was a good dancer. Better than their husbands. And his pleasure was infectious.

When he returned from his military service, he was eager to meet women at the dances. He would arrive with two or three of his mates from the village. The other guys were not so keen. As they entered the hall, they could tell that the women were already looking down at them. They made crude jokes and shuffled their feet. Slowly, slowly one or the other of the guys would slip away. Louis would always be one of the last to leave, but he too would return to his car, which he cleaned earlier in the day, and go home on his own.

In his childhood the boys were awkward with the girls. At school and church, they were kept apart. At home, they were given different jobs. A wall of ignorance was put between them. Banter was rare, even between brother and sister.

When my mother was attracted to a man in the *kafenion* it was taboo to even exchange a single word. With her girlfriend Sophia on her left shoulder, they would do the *volta* – anti-clockwise laps of the square. As they approached the glass window of the *kafenion* she would raise her glance. He would lift his left eyebrow as he held his cards tight to his chest. That was enough. She knew she could not be seen with him because her uncle would have never approved it. Instead, she arranged for messages to be exchanged and they agreed to meet in Australia. She dreamed that in a new country love could happen like it did in the songs and movies.

Louis was happy to dance even if the women had eyes for elsewhere.

In his youth he experienced numerous rejections. His clothes were clean, but the women had an eye for minor details. Before leaving his parent's home he would stare at the solitary mirror in the bathroom, ask advice from Lina, his elder sister. If he had a wife, she would know what he should wear. In his middle age he chose carefully. Nothing flash. He did not pretend to understand fashions. He only wanted to appear acceptable: to have the whiff of straw and old milk far from his skin.

His sister would soon join the gendered exodus and leave the village to marry a shopkeeper. She did not want to walk with sabots rimmed with mud. His parents had nothing to say about fashion and dances. They accepted that a girl could leave for the city, but the boy must stay to keep the cows. The thought of talking about appearances, let alone going together to the dance, never crossed his father's mind. Nothing could be more embarrassing.

The other peasant boys had resigned themselves. They knew that they could not dance. Hanging around was pointless. They felt goofy and no amount of washing could take the smell of the barn out of their skin. When one did dare to step out, the other boys laughed and were quick to point out the number of times the girl's toes were trodden on. They ridiculed each other. Louis should have given up. He knew that dancing was foreign. Everything in the hall was the opposite of the farm. The other boys were right. They were brought up to dread the idea of putting themselves on display. A peasant is not taught to adorn their body. None of this was natural for Louis. He was caught in a bundle of competing nerves. Shyness to cover his injured pride, but also the delight of dancing allowed him to leap over the fear of rejection. He learned by looking closely at the men who came from the city. First the foxtrot, the Charleston, the cha-cha, and later even a bit of salsa. When he danced there were no awkward lunges or gauche steps.

Women were a mystery to Louis. Lina dreamed of the new fashions and clean houses. She found independence in the town. Her husband was paid fortnightly regardless of the weather or the health of cows. The jobs in the city were hard, but they were secure. His sister wanted to buy new clothes and not sit with her mother to make them. A man with seventeen cows and three houses could not compete with this. His routine had not changed for centuries. Lina, by contrast, was free to visit on weekends.

Eventually, Louis accepted that he was 'unmarriageable'. He never spoke of his frustrations. Even though the dice were loaded to embarrass him, he found the courage to keep coming back to the dances. I noticed that while he danced with ease, he seldom chatted with his dancing partners. Was this for fear of crossing a line, or a consequence of the closure of his own emotional walls? Louis's discretion was also a space of freedom for the women who danced with him. They knew that he was not a gossip and that he would always be at the dances.

Louis also played the saxophone. At night, if he noticed that Yves and I were coming up the hill, he would start on Hadjidakis's tune for the film *Never on a Sunday*. I am not sure who in the village would have taught him how to play, or whether he learned it during his military service. He did not go hunting or keep a gun in the house. Sometimes he played in the kitchen with the door open to the cows in the stable, at other times by the front door. His house was at the top of the village. Where did those notes go?

Laurie Anderson sang a song that claimed that the music transmitted from a radio antenna achieved immortality. Those notes travel endlessly on radio waves, across the night skies of the cosmos, and bounce back and forth to earth.

Music comes from far away. Yet, it arrives as if it were already inside you. When you sway and dance to music there is an exemption from time, and a duel with the forces of gravity. It grabs the imagination and unleashes the wildness in you. Your body demands to be let free.

In John's story 'The Accordion Player' an admirer gushes: 'I love music! With music you can say everything!'

'You cannot talk to a lawyer with music.'

The reply by the accordion-playing peasant was straight out of the wry mouth of Louis.

During haymaking Louis drove a German Mengele tractor with two attachments. If there were no rain interruptions all the hay could be brought into the barn in eight or ten days. A windrower is used to make the first cut, and a tedder for fluffing the grass to help it dry.

My parents also worked the fields. The ground was tilled, and the irrigation channels were shaped by long-handle hoes. Spades were rare and confined to those with vineyards. Ploughs and harrows were shared. During the harvest period they worked with scythes, wooden rakes and pitchforks. My mother would rake, her brother Nikiforo would flick the hay with a fork onto the cart, and their Uncle Simeon would build the stack. They inserted a pike between the wooden spokes to keep the cart from sliding on the grass.

When I first came to help John passed me a wooden rake to claw back the grass that landed on the verge. I immediately pulled too hard on the knotted grass and broke the rake. I couldn't read the flow and the tool was a generation away from being attached to my body.

The timing of the harvest was always a gamble. Louis wanted to cut the grass when it reached its maximum height, but he also needed a sufficient window of clear days so that he could turn it and allow it to dry before it rained. If we stored the grass while it was damp, there was the risk it would ferment, losing its nutrients and possibly starting a fire in the barn. For Louis the harvest was an anxious time.

After Louis gathered the dry grass, he would dump it all at the entrance to the barn. That is where Yves, John and I stood. With pitchforks in hand, we would load a machine that spewed the grass up into the attic of the barn. The young Yves would be in the top section, steering the funnel so that the grass would fall as neatly as possible in between the rafters. Yves started with the corners, slowly filling the middle, ending each shift with a swan dive from the rafters onto the freshly laid hay. As the hay climbed up the cathedral the little beams of light that came in through the holes in the wooden planks would be plugged and darkness gathered. It was hot, ticklish and dusty work. We wore surgical masks that I had purchased in London from a Harley Street chemist. (The only other request John sent through was to pack in my panniers two jars of Horlicks malt milk powder.) In between the loads, Yves would scramble down from the loft, and in our moments of respite we would play pigeon-toss – throwing coins against the wall. The coins were stored in a jar. Savings from the trips before the Euro was the only currency. We would take five steps back from the barn and shoot. The one closest would win a bottle of *Châteauneuf-du-Pape* at the end of the campaign. The year Scott came he would use his 'Inspector Gadget' long arms and win a bit too easily.

On my first road trip to Quincy, I followed the route that John would take across France. He would traverse the country on the small Department roads, Calais, Lens, Cambrai, Saint-Quentin, Soissons, Troyes, along the Seine River to Dijon then over the Jura Mountains to Geneva and, finally the home straight to Mieussy. John resisted taking any of the toll highways. 'That would be boring. All you do is count the miles like a prisoner, carving notches on a wall to measure the days.'

As I rode from one village roundabout through to the next, and admired the quaint stone houses, appreciated the care with which the potted geranium flowers were hung on balconies, and counted out the diminishing proximity to Paris, I often asked myself, why not live here, why did John choose to be so far from the centre, and why so high up the mountains?

As I approached Quincy, I noticed something different. There was a roughness to the sun-blackened pine timber used on the barns; a restraint in the use of floral decorations; a severity in the granite and limestone mountain edges. This landscape seemed to resonate with the black humour, and the design rivalled the stoic nature, of the villagers.

When the haymaking was finished the barn smelled of fresh toast. With a huge sigh Louis would announce, as if for the first time, that we should gather for a celebratory dinner at a restaurant in Laitraz that was just above the village of Saint-Denis. In the past, this was a ritual in which the young, who had worked hard in the harvest, would gather. Now it was mostly older people. Louis would be on a high and only then he would gently mutter, '*nous ne somme de partis les plus malheureux au monde*' – we are not amongst the most miserable in the world. After the meal Yves and I got up to dance. A neighbour, who moved to the nearby town of Saint-Jeoire, left her drunken husband, who was slouched over the table, and joined us. Her eyes were full of the delight of a sky-blue escape.

John had found people he could believe in. They also found in him a person that doesn't just 'write-talk-lies write-talk-lies write-talk-lies' but was willing to sweat beside them. It was in the work of the harvest that friendship was first forged in the village. When Louis fixed his machines, John would fetch tools. He would scramble in the barn to find where Louis last left the wrench. John could put in a screw and hammer a nail, but he had no idea how different mechanical parts worked together. In the field he worked as hard as the peasants. When Louis spoke at the kitchen table, John's ears pricked up. John's attention to Louis's words was a soothing presence.

My mother and father worked hard in the Greek village. They

worked even harder in the Australian factories. But on the weekends, they danced and sang. It was one of their disappointments that their 'successful' sons would sit around a dinner table, exchange opinions, and call this entertainment. When they danced the floorboards shook. Hips swivelled. Ankles tapped. Knees close together. Dexterity and decorum in harmony. My uncle Nikiforo's sister-in-law worked in a shop, but she wanted to be an artist. She had dark curly hair and blue eyes. When she danced the kids stopped sliding through the legs of the adults. In platform cork shoes and bell-bottom jeans, she danced so vigorously that it would wrinkle up and bulge open the linoleum floor covering. Little drops of sweat would trickle down her temples. Between songs she would wave her hand as if it were a fan, and then launch herself again.

My uncles danced with a cigarette dangling from their lips. My father never smoked, and I never got used to the bitter burning taste. When the room got thick, I went outside. I tilted my head back and stared up towards the full moon, and the stars that sparkled over the southern skies. I wished that I could climb up on the red terracotta roof tiles, feel the rumble from the party beneath and the humming of the cosmos above.

Mountain water was plentiful in the Haute-Savoie. There was a fountain on the side of the road going to Louis's house. On some occasions we rested near the trough where the cows drank the water that came straight out of the springs. John and I splashed our faces. Simon McBurney stripped down and plunged in.

John often talked about the consciousness of cycles in the peasant mindset. 'They don't memorialise the past like beads in a necklace, but rather remember as they plant, harvest, prune and renew. Their distrust towards the promises of the future was born from a recognition that uncertainty engulfed the certitudes of progress.' The tractor was the beginning of the end. He referred to 'life as an interlude', and as for the inescapable death, he would chuckle as he quoted a saying in the village: 'shut my umbrella at night'.

Simon surfaced from the trough, barrel-chested and immortal.

John and I sat in the shade of the shed. The shed was in the shade of a large tree, which itself was in the shadow of the mountain.

I asked John: 'You have ancestry that takes you to Trieste, the region where part of the novel *G* was set, you live part of the year with Nella in Paris, you lived in the Forest of Dean where you wrote that miraculous book on a country doctor, and you were raised in South London. When you die, where do you want to be buried?'

He replied: 'Right here in Quincy.'

The afternoon coolness spread across Louis's farm. I looked at John as he stared towards the road. A little trickle of sweat rolled from his temple towards his orange-and-red kerchief. His naked arms, blue singlet and the long green grass swam in harmony. We felt that the mountains had embraced us. Our bodies were inside something vast.

Louis rumbled towards us on his tractor. It was his last load before dinner. The jagged lines of the mountain peaks came closer. We pushed up off the ground and moved back to our positions at the mouth of the barn. We had one more load of hay to feed into the barn.

More than twenty years later I came back to the village. I had missed John's funeral. I wanted to pay my respects to Yves and Katya. Chloe the first grandchild was now a beautiful Greek-looking young woman. She was living with Katya in Geneva. Yves and Sandra had a son and a daughter. John was buried next to Beverly in Église Saint-Gervais, Mieussy.

If you had a strong arm, you could pluck an apple from the tree just below Louis's house and fling it down the hill so that it landed on John's roof. Well, maybe, but not quite. The distance, as the crow flies, is quite small. However, the road to Louis's house is long. It meanders up the hill and then loops around. Walking is slow, so after lunch we would jump in the little red Renault and arrive before he dumped his first load of hay.

There was a private road that bisected Louis's fields. Elm trees lined this road, and he let the grass and wildflowers grow along the verge and in between the tyre tracks. Sprinkled in the fields were copses with large oak and linden trees. There were also the larches and Arollas – a pine tree that is distinctive to the region.

The British artist Stephen Willats observed that the kids living in the lumpen British suburbs would make refuges in the nooks of housing estates and along the edges of the crofts in the abandoned public spaces. In these 'lurky places' they took drugs and fantasised about other lives. Defying the gravity of concrete brutalism and hidden from surveillant eyes they got high and laughed at the words that tumbled from their mouths.

We only made hay on sunny days. As we drove along the private road we would notice, but never discussed, an elderly couple that picnicked in the shade. He was silver-haired and portly. She was tall and blonde. They were both well-tanned. She had an endless range of leopard and tiger printed bikinis. They were not from the village. I imagine it was a secret amorous escape. John uttered a complicit grunt as we drove by, and Louis always looked the other way. We all pretended as if they had put up a magic screen.

When desire comes it floods. It is such an effort to hold it back and keep your balance. What pain must be generated by the conflict between the rush of desire and the need to keep your control. The passion in Louis was kept silent. I never heard him complain or vent.

Louis only walks to gather his cows. Everywhere else he drives. The dairy where he deposits his milk is five kilometres away. He would not take a walk to visit a neighbour or take in some air. Everyone is busy.

If Louis encounters any stranger, he will notice everything: age, dress style, marital status, possibly even place of origin. But most of all he remains discreet. His eyes do not linger. Even if the strangers are passing him on his own road he acts as if they will never meet again. To acknowledge the strangers would remove their camouflage. Intrude on the delight of escape. Even when the glances of different eyes meet, his gaze must remain suspended in the void beyond. This is the contract he has with himself and the sunbathers. He craves to see her flesh. But this can only happen if time stops. Normally, she will notice the rumbling of his tractor's approach. As he passes, he feigns to avert his gaze. His eyes are as innocent as the birds above and the rabbits below. They will pretend to skip past the hint of a cleavage hidden in the tall grasses.

The midday sun is doing its furnace work. Louis has turned the cut grass. It is becoming juicy and crisp. The golden part of the afternoon is about to commence. The shadows start to stretch. The sun dips into a copper colour. The valley cools. The greens become subdued by the creeping blue-black evening. At the end of the day, we will slip down the hill, shower and prepare our evening feast. Louis will go into the kitchen and warm up his leftovers.

While the red pot is on the oven Louis steps back into the stable. He fondles a few stalks that feed his cows. The rhythm of the house and barn quietens. He crosses back into his kitchen and turns on the TV. He is not expecting anyone. The front door is open. He looks down the corridor and sees a beam of moonlight. There is no wind tonight and so the owl stalks with extra lightness. Louis is weary. His physical tiredness and his contemplation of the day have not found a balance. His right hand runs along the course threads of his trousers. Some nights he feels like sleeping with his boots on.

The fierceness of the evening birdsong is in hiatus. There are nights when even this is inaudible to Louis. It took me years to notice the cascading sequences and the rivalrous counterpoints. The trees in front of Louis's house were full of birds. On some nights the music of birdsong blurred the edges.

Who made that whistle?

It is coming up the hill.

Another note.

Slightly muffled this time.

It is closer. Somewhere between the apple and the pear tree.

The next whistle is accompanied by a giggle. It was Yves practising the whistling technique I had taught him earlier in the day. Louis half-smiled. Yves came into Louis's house with no purpose in mind. A crow cawed three times. Yves sat down at the kitchen table for a few minutes. Then he got up to take Louis's empty dinner plate to the sink, gather the loose crumbs in his open palm and sprinkle them on the grass beyond the entrance. He then went back down the hill still trying to get the whistling right.

Louis returns to his solitude as the bridge of the whistling fades. He tries to imagine the world – and in particular, the world without him. Today the fields had been cut in neat lines. The hay is ascending towards the cathedral. If he were outside the stars would be there and the full cream moon would be pricked by the sharp edges of the alps. Louis turns off the TV as the alert newsreader begins his report. He pauses in the afterglow of the blue screen light. Outside a shooting star flickers past and everyone misses it.

John felt a little bit of pride that his presence in the village kept the postman coming and the alcohol inspector from discovering the secret *gnole* in everyone's cellar.

The Guardian, Le Monde diplomatique, El País, The New Yorker, and letters with exotic stamps arrived daily. John was a passionate correspondent – his letters to Subcomandante Marcos were the stuff of legends and his exchange with Leon Kossoff contains the most brilliant comparison between the warm production in a kitchen and the life in an artist's studio. He laughed at the cartoons in *The New Yorker*, but I don't remember seeing him read the papers. Maybe he saved that for the bog.

Beverly read the news assiduously. Gently drawing on her cigarette, or sipping her coffee, as she turned each page, slowly. She savoured her solitude in the garden with cigarettes and tissue-thin newspapers.

She raised her eyes above her glasses as a blackbird dropped onto the fence line. The blackberries were almost ripe.

'Shoo. Shoo.'

Even when she was trying to be hostile her voice was soft and silky. The blackbird remained oblivious, and his feathers glistened in the clean sun. It hopped a few steps closer to the fruit.

Beverly got up from her seat and waved the finger armed with the glowing cigarette at its tip. The blackbird reluctantly relinquished its territory.

Beverly is not so territorial as to wrap the bushes with a protective net, but she needs the berries to make cassis. Above the rooftop three swallows are whirling in the thermals and feasting on the summer band of mosquitoes. Beverly pretends not to notice. The red roof tiles are all straight. The metal snow guards are bolted tight to the gutters. The light-blue shutters have been freshly painted. Once again Beverly raises her eyes above the rim of her glass and wonders about the audacity of birds.

'If everything they need is already up there, why come down?'

Beverly drank her filtered coffee in a mug. Yves and John followed the local custom of a small bowl. This bowl was not designed to be carried to your desk, it was open, the coffee swirled and cooled sooner. John drank it quickly, upright, and got back to work.

When I was a child in Melbourne, we would visit friends and family on weekends. Before the kids were allowed to run out and play on the street, there was a civil period where we were received in the immaculate living room. We sat quietly on the new couches in our clean clothes. The parents made small talk, we were offered sweetened figs, nuts and sometimes, sweet chewy *masticha* was served on a long spoon in a tall glass of water. For our parents, Chiclet-style chewing gum *tzichles* and other sugary things did not come to their village until well after the war. *Masticha* came from the trees on the island of Chios. While the parents talked the kids remained frozen in a show of best behaviour. I would daydream, stare at the collection of Czech crystal glasses, lock eyes with the hideous monstera plant in the corner which I was convinced my aunt nurtured in the hope that one night it would unfurl its wicked leaves and swallow my snoring uncle, and into the bargain, I would add, her conniving young son, but most of all, I remained puzzled at how a full-sized pear had been seamlessly squeezed into a large bottle of liqueur.

On the sunny crest of Louis's hill there were a few fruit trees. A dozen bottles hung off the branches. Someone had threaded the flowering buds through the neck until it was halfway into the stomach of each bottle. At first, I guessed that René Magritte did not have far to go. As Yves walked by, I asked him what fruit grew on these trees. He saw my eyes following the bobbing of the bottles in the gentle early summer breeze and chuckled: 'pears'.

The alcohol inspector made periodic but unannounced visits to the region. From Saint-Jeoire the fast-running Giffre River keeps pace with the cars alongside on the D907. Even in the spring the river seems shallow and icy grey. Turning onto the D226 the road squiggles around the small Lac d'Anthon where the woodchoppers stack their logs, and then it straightens as you pass the smaller village of Ley. John's house was the first in the village of Quincy and at that point the road makes a hairpin turn. The inspector was also a fan of John's novels.

She usually arrived in the afternoon and John would immediately offer coffee. Her hands were soft and clean. She had a pleasant smile and was well-dressed. Nevertheless, she was the representative of the state – the greatest thief! John did not seek the attention of adoring fans, but during this coffee break, he would bring out his latest manuscript. Meanwhile Yves would mount his bike and warn all the neighbours to stash the stills and camouflage the demijohns of *gnole* – *eau de vie* – water of life, fifty-per-cent-proof moonshine. The *gnole* was made from the dregs – *marc* – of pressed apple cider.

By the time she left, everyone was smiling, happy to play cat-and-mouse with the inspector. They enjoyed pretending to be proud to be on the right of the law, but most of all they hated the thought that they would have to pay tax on a product that they produced for their own pleasure, and which, after all, was also useful as an antiseptic, helped preserve fruit, and dulled the pain for their animals.

Peasants were always against something. Before their contempt for the state there was suspicion of the church. They knew that priests were either lazy hypocrites or busy at being promiscuous parasites. During the wars patriots and revolutionaries made great speeches, but it was the peasants that did most of the fighting and endured the long hungry cold nights in the trenches. Some people thought that the peasants were anarchists, but peasants were also opposed to anarchism.

Although Louis owned the house that John lived in, he was not that interested in the income from the rent. However, what he was most appreciative of was the help to bring in the hay. And, of course, the companionship.

John greeted him as *patron*. The one who decides, the one who is in charge.

By contrast Louis called John *le comédien*, by which he meant that John was part bohemian and part travelling player. He would toy with John, getting him to guess the weather, as if he were asking permission as to when he should cut the grass. If John got it wrong, he would say, 'Hah! You're just a comedian.' If John got it right, then he would claim that it was he who decided anyway.

Louis was younger than John. Lina, his elder sister, would visit occasionally armed with cherry tart. It was in equal measure delicious and dangerous – the pips were never removed. She would be busy in the kitchen. A bit manic but with no hint of nostalgia. Her daughters giggled and pretended to be helpful. Louis adored his nieces, but Yves was his favourite.

When Louis greeted us, he would squint and lift his blue cap. John would do the same. Louis wore a flannel shirt and a white singlet underneath. John had a blue singlet and red kerchief around his neck. Louis's arms were tanned, but from his open shirt you could see that his chest and back were as pale as a baby's. John loved to sunbathe, and he wore blue trousers, the same that were issued to the council road workers.

Work was punctuated by moments of rest. During these breaks Louis would bring out bread, Tomme – the local hard cheese – and because he knew I liked it very much, a small wheel of the soft and tangy Reblochon. He would unfold the Opinel knives that were also made in the Haute-Savoie region, gently cut the rind from the Tomme and slice the bread.

The kitchen was cool in the summer and warm in the winter. It always had the slightly milky-sour smell of labour. There were no more than one set of plates waiting to be washed in the sink. It took me a few seasons to notice that there was no bin in the house. The crumbs were gathered and tossed outside. Whatever fell was ground into the planks of wood. Everything, everything was recycled!

John would ask Louis serious questions. What is the future of the EU? Will it rain tomorrow? Did Le Pen have a chance in the region? Louis watched the news and did not believe in John's barometer. He looked and listened carefully. His answers to John's questions were pithy. After he spoke, John would underline the point with a sequence of ascending assents:

Oui.

Oui.

Ouuiii.

However, John was also concerned about the difficulties of living alone. As Teodor Shanin observed in the documentary on *Pig Earth* – John was learning from 'old men who had no sons to teach'. Louis was destined to be a bachelor. John suggested that they place a personal ad in the *Country Weekly News*. Jean Mohr agreed to take the portrait and John wrote a brief bio in haiku.

Traditionally, when a marriage was arranged it was not just a matter of whether the two individuals made a good couple. It involved the intertwining of two families, and therefore, everyone was part of the calculation. Lineage was as important as personal character. Having good and reliable cousins improved your stocks. Feeling was a minor part of the decision. John was, inadvertently, playing a modern variation on the role that Pierre Bourdieu described as the *traqueur* – the arranger. Louis looked at him with a mixture of disdain and ironic distance. There were no women in the village to be introduced to. Lina had left. His family tree had shrunk. He was on his own.

When the advertisement was placed Louis got very nervous. He turned to John and said:

'I am not interested in a widow – she might have killed the man.

I am not interested in a divorcee – she might leave me too.

I am not interested in a spinster – she might be the reason no one else is interested in her.

I am not interested in a young wife – she will cuckold me for sure.'

'But Louis, that eliminates everyone!' replied John.

The all-encompassing symmetry of his caveats was startling. It was a hermetic system that was tinged with hurt and pride. Despite his loneliness Louis was still driven by a code that he should not marry beneath himself. After all he had three houses with a view of Mont Blanc. But there was a quiet anguish in his negation. Louis would cut the grass in his fields in precise straight lines, but the order with which he stored the tools in his garage was a mystery that no one else could decode. Everything was exactly where he last left it, but the curse that you would hear most often, was, *singe travail* – monkey work! Even this little curse was muttered almost silently under the muffle of his moustache.

The Savoyards seem to chew their curses. By contrast, if you open your window in a Greek village, whether it was because a cat was passing, or, even worse, a priest, something or someone was being cursed at any time of the day. A Greek can curse with variety and dexterity. It can either appear in short blasts or escalate into a full opera that includes the relatives, saints, Christ, his mother, the Holy Spirit and not even stopping at God. By the time the Greek has stopped cursing, the offence has long passed, and everything can resume as before. Louis could not imagine cursing in front of a woman. He was not that religious, but he would never dare bring up the Virgin Mary. In French and English one of the lowest of curses is to call a woman a cow. This just shows how detached people in the city are from the countryside. Cows are the loveliest of animals.

Louis was persuaded to look at the responses to the advertisement in the *Country Weekly News*. Eventually, he plucked the courage to contact one. After a brief correspondence the woman agreed to meet him. She would come with her mother and stay for the weekend in Louis's guest house.

Louis tidied up everything beautifully. John brought flowers to freshen the kitchen. After so many years as a bachelor Louis had resigned himself to living in a functional manner. There were no images on the walls. All the furniture was either inherited from his parents or there for a purpose. His house was substantial. It was not like the single-storey dwelling of the sharecroppers. He had a large sideboard for displaying china plates and a solid wooden bed. However, he had not learned the art of turning the house into a home. When the car pulled up John was smiling but Louis was sweating. The conversation seemed to be going well, so after the coffee John walked home. Later in the afternoon Louis asked to be excused so that he could go to milk the cows.

The woman and her mother expressed an interest in going down and taking a closer look at Mieussy. The shops hugged a narrow ridge. The *tabac* and post office were on one side, the café and baker on the other. On the higher side was the church and a restaurant with an inn. The big houses, where the mayor tended to reside, were along this elevated point. When John first arrived in Quincy, there was still a café in the village. It sold souvenirs – snow domes, fold-up knives and miniature cow bells. The sign is still visible, as is the cross on the entrance to the tiny church across the road. Louis would rarely go into Mieussy. He had neither the time nor the inclination to go to the café and play cards. He gave directions to Mieussy and they walked back towards their car that was parked next to the guest house.

Louis changed into his crusty working clothes and went into the stable to milk the cows. His routine could not change. Even in the summer he went out with the cows each morning. Cleaned the stable. Cut wood for the winter. Did some minor repairs. Brought the cows back from the fields. Attached the machine to their udders, cleaned out the barn, and then deposited the milk at the dairy.

When I took that first step from his kitchen to the barn it was the ammonia in the cow's piss that pinched my nose. A cow pisses thirteen litres and drops a barrowful of shit every day. Louis shovelled the shit onto a heap behind the barn and would spray the fields with it. In Homer's *Odyssey* a similar practice is recorded. The cow's shit is heaped outside the gates and then spread on the fields. A cow patty on its own is heavy. If left on the grass nothing would grow under it. I never discovered the sweetness in the smell of their shit. But after a few days I stopped noticing it.

After Louis finished in the barn, he hosed down the entrance, and washed himself up. He warmed the dinner that he had prepared the night before and set the table. He brought out a tablecloth that Lina had given to him and lit three candles. As the quietness of night approached, he started to worry. The car had not returned from Mieussy. He walked up to the guest house and saw that the suitcases had been taken.

'For a century and a half now the tenacious ability of peasants to survive has confounded administrators and theorists. Today it can still be said that the majority in the world are peasants. Yet this fact masks a more significant one. For the first time ever it is possible that the class of survivors may not survive. Within a century there may be no more peasants. In Western Europe, if the plans work out as the economic planners have foreseen, there will be no more peasants within twenty-five years.'

This is from the opening paragraph to *Pig Earth*. It was published in 1979. By the turn of the century, on schedule, the prediction had been fulfilled. At the beginning of the nineteenth century only fifteen per cent of the French people were urban and eighty-five per cent were peasants. The twentieth century began by flipping this ratio in France. By the turn of the twenty-first century all the peasants were gone. My parents had moved from their peasant villages in Greece and become proletarians in the factories of Australia. Their 'class', which had 'survived' thousands of years of imperial domination, religious wars, feudalism and colonisation, was now finally wiped out. Modernity, with the appeal of labour-saving devices and individual progress, erased the need for peasants.

In the summer Louis would take his cows to the higher pastures on his farm. When they came down the hill there was something unharmonious about their sauntering descent. Their heads and tails would sway in unison. However, if one of the cows picked up the pace, there was a dreadful sense that she might topple, and all the others would tumble after her. Their thin legs seemed incomplete for their large frames.

If Louis was given the chance to design their hooves, he would have removed the stilettos – that cut into the damp path – and replaced them with wide sensible boots. He would not touch their eyes, as they were the reason he gave them beautiful names such as Celeste, Estelle and Corine.

John, Yves and I waited at the bottom of the hill. We would stare at the muddy path and hope no one slipped. To be on the safe side we kept away from the wall. The cows knew their silent path back to the stable. Yves enjoyed patting their spotted hide. John wondered how much longer this precarious world could last.

When I arrived in 1993 Louis was the last person still farming by the old peasant ways in Quincy. As John got older, he spent more time in Paris. Yves continued to help. They managed to carry on until Louis had a heart attack. When he left the village to go to the hospital the cows were sold. By the time I returned in 2017 the barn had been empty for years. The long drooping muzzles, that kept each cow in place and prevented them from eating the straw on their bedding, the tools that Louis had put down thinking that he might need it again the next day, and the smell of cow's piss, it was all still there. Near the entrance were crates of plastic bottles waiting to be filled with *gnole*, and two trays of potatoes. Some empty champagne bottles still hung around the side door to the kitchen. It felt as if the cows had just gone out to the pasture. Morning light was coming through the holes formed by the knots of the wood planks and the windows at the far end. A clean shovel and broom rested against the rusted generator.

A subsistence farmer makes enough from this earth to exist. There is almost no waste, and any surplus is reserved for festivities. My father took great care in how much water he used for his vegetables in Melbourne. Even when water consumption was not measured, he would say: 'Only use enough so that there is some for those who have so little.' It was as if he were still drawing water from a river that had to give to others further downstream. We are not alone and what we have in this world is not a possession.

7. The Son Who Stayed

Winters are long in the Alps. When the barn is full the day's work is not so demanding. Feeding the cows, sluicing away the shit and milking still leaves you with some time.

That is how the cuckoo clock was invented.

In the in-between hours and long nights men would tinker with cogs, springs and chains. Over generations fine motor skills were honed. In *The Third Man* Orson Welles delivered a cruel joke about the sum of the Swiss contribution to Western civilisation.

There was a cuckoo clock above the fireplace. But it had not sung in years.

Social life in Quincy was quiet and discreet. There was attention but it was never obtrusive. When Mano moved into the house next door, it was not a surprise to hear that he was an engineer specialising in the production of fine aeronautical components – the valley was now a world leader in making tiny mechanical parts that were like those once used in a cuckoo clock.

Mano, with his spiky punk black hair and pastel-coloured Benetton shirts, managed one of the factories in Cluses. Skills that were once refined by hand as a hobby in the kitchen, were now automated and distributed across a production line. The only pay-off – four weeks annual summer leave. The houses in the surrounding villages, that were once the epicentre of a working life, were slowly reduced to dormitories.

The old neighbours never knocked on the door during working hours. If they did, you could be sure that they either needed something – some sugar for the cassis – or that it was an emergency – Come quick, fire!

In the early evening the broad-shouldered, taciturn and well-tanned Andre would often show up. He ran a holiday camp for the kids in the working-class suburbs of Paris. His son Giles was a famous naturalist photographer and an extreme mountain climber. His daughter Chrystal was a bank official and as beautiful as Brigitte Bardot. Andre was a widow. Handsome and thoughtful. There was a dignified solemnity to him, and it felt as if nothing frivolous ever came from his lips. He had a calming influence on John as they shared a pre-dinner pastis and ice.

Mano, by contrast, was the ever-ready enthusiast. He was a bit too cheerful. At nights and on weekends he wanted to be involved with the village. His wife was at home all day but less visible. He was knocking on the door all the time. Forever boasting about the benefits brought on by the aeronautical firm. When he heard about the midsummer rituals, he immediately wanted to take charge. Yves and the boys from Ley were much younger than Mano. It might be because he was full of management speak, but they resented his tempo and determination to take the lead. It made them indignant. Some things, like love and football, are better off without money and managers. The boys decided to go slow. They didn't dislike Mano. He was a nice guy. But their fancy dress and fireworks parties did not need to be organised on a spreadsheet and scheduled in a Filofax. Even the teenagers were suspicious of what was coming their way.

It was on the evening of my first visit to Quincy. We were at a restaurant. Yves was like a frisky pup. We had unloaded our heavy coats in the alcove by the door and the big red pot of fondue was about to arrive.

Beverly whispered. Yves shuddered. John stiffened.

I was puzzled.

Beverly repeated: 'Boarding school.'

She giggled, neither Yves nor John was amused.

Beverly turned to me and explained that this was the nuclear deterrent that was used to keep Yves from misbehaving when they went out. When I was eighteen, I toured California with the Victorian Schoolboy Rugby Team. We were billeted in the houses of the opposing teams. My host in San Francisco took me home to meet his mum, whom he described, as he was pulling a carton of eggnog from the fridge, as easy! He took his swig, showed me my room, and then raced off to yet another concert by the Grateful Dead. Beverly was easygoing. John not so with his young son, who was always running, fidgeting, bumping into things, and in general just could not sit still.

However, Yves's head was already filled with the horror stories of John's boarding-school experiences in England. The cold showers. The hierarchy of fags. The flashing cane. The shit-sandwiches. And the sleeping in a room with twenty other whimpering boys.

He never complained about waking up before his parents and taking a bus to the school in Cluses. The school was a formidable five-storey stone building with a high wrought-iron gate. In the winter it seemed cold and severe. Even in the summer the massive stone edifice looked damp. Yves probably thought that it could be worse, much worse! He sat without rocking his chair in the restaurant.

It was rare to eat out. In the summer we enjoyed the pleasure of preparing a meal for the family. My specialty was lamb and pork souvlaki. Bauge, the butcher in Mieussy, would dice the meat perfectly. He was as tall as a lineout jumper in a rugby team but dressed like a dandy. As he cut the meat with his finely sharpened knives, he gave precise instructions on temperature and duration. I would skewer the lamb and pork in an alternating order. Then marinate them overnight with chopped onions, oregano, salt, pepper, olive oil and whatever was left over in the unlabelled bottles of Beaujolais.

After we returned from haymaking John and Yves would take a shower and I would light the fire in the small pit. As the wood turned to hot embers and it was time to put the skewers on the grill, I would sneak into the *cave* and pull out a handful of dried vine clippings. This final touch to the fire added a wine-scented smoke.

John was the quickest out of the shower. He would sit by the white garden table and announce: 'The jumps just got higher.'

After the meal, as the coals lost their red heat, he would throw in three or four *melitzanes*. By next morning they had been smoked to a squidgy perfection. He peeled off the charcoaled skin and then scooped the fruit into a bowl with garlic, parsley, olive oil and yoghurt. To me, any dish from Sicily to Syria is delicious. The Mediterranean is only one per cent of the world's surface, but as Perry Anderson said, it was the most improbable conductor of civilisation. Unlike the land-trekking armies, the carriage of ideas and commerce was mostly by sea.

However, there was no doubt over the culinary prize-winner. When Yves was seventeen, he started dating Sandra. She was working in a local supermarket and was also friends with the boys from the village of Ley. Sandra had a wisdom beyond her years and was a marvellous cook. She trumped the season by slow-cooking a chicken encased in rock salt. When she pulled the steel pot from the oven the salt looked like a dome of frozen crystals. She took a large spoon, stabbed the sloping white crust with the pointy end and below was a perfectly tanned chook. Succulent heaven.

'Gold prize,' declared John.

'Yves, EEEEves, Yves!!!!'

'Yes, Papa.'

Whether as an adult or as a boy, any softness in Yves's voice and John would melt. He was sensitive to tone and the slightest glimpse of pain. A single tear welling up in the other's eye and he could drown. John could flip from being an Alsatian to a wide-eyed Cavalier. With Nella he purred around the house. In Quincy he was protective. He always called Beverly 'luv'. It sounded a bit quaint and old-fashioned to my Australian ears. But he would lose it when Beverly, unhappy with his first answer, would ask the same question in three different ways.

As a young boy Yves and his bike were in everybody's house and garden. He was unstoppable.

In the nights we would take long walks. Heading past Louis's house, then up towards Saint-Denis, looping around the ridge and down to Ley. At times, we would see lightning flicker around the mountain tops and echo along the valleys. With this syncopated delivery it was hard to tell from the delay between sight and sound whether it was near or far. We would sprint the last straight section.

Yves would confide his struggles and the ancient Greek phrase *midén ágan* – no excess – resonated for both of us, not in a conservative and repressive way, but as a recognition of the difficulty of reconciling impulses with reflection. The interplay between thought and experience was never smooth. It became a motto for the walks. Yves and I dissected our fears and flaws. I marvelled at his sweetness and the kindness of his soul. At times I thought that the moon was altering its course so that the path before us was well lit.

When Beverly gave birth to Yves there were no other babies in the village. Everyone treated him as if he were their youngest. It was customary for fathers to be rough with their eldest son, but even Louis giggled when Yves was either late or distracted.

Yves was always conscious that his father was old. It was rare in the village for a man to have a child at the age of fifty. Yves wondered to himself:

'Will I still have a father when I am ten? What will it be like when he is seventy and I will be twenty?'

Yves did not expect John to be with him when he turned forty. He was also conscious that his father was famous.

'I grew up knowing that I had to share him with the world.'

The Spanish painter Miquel Barceló came often to the village. We never overlapped, but his catalogues were often at the edge of the table. John wrote an essay for one of them. Barceló invited Yves to spend a week in his Paris studio. On his return Yves was still giddy with the thrill of it. His bag was triumphant – full of ochres, pigments, charcoals and papers. He was a little singed by the sexual frisson in the art world. He felt a bit confused with the hints of charming intimacy and the dead weight of objectification.

Most of all Yves was enthralled by the metamorphosis of materials.

There is a portrait of John by Barceló in their former pigsty which is now a library. The textures and colours in his face echo the splintered contours and glint in the landscape.

Drawing and painting were done after the haymaking, or on wet days. Later, Yves enrolled at the art school in Geneva. It was the same art school that Jimmie Durham attended. Beverly wanted Yves to go to Paris, or even further. I was a guest lecturer at the Glasgow School of Art. From fear of backlash John remained reserved on the topic. He took comfort and expressed gratitude in private when I pushed Yves to go to Glasgow. John chuckled when I told them of the glass corridor at the top of the Mackintosh building in Glasgow. When the building first opened, male and female students were segregated. It was only along the glass 'hen run' that they met. Yves had no desire to leave Louis, the cows, the village, his home. John was becoming too old to help Louis. Yves gladly did more and more of the work. He enrolled at the *beaux-arts* and commuted to Geneva in muddy boots. The barn in John's house is now Yves's studio. He goes there to lose his ego.

In a letter he told me: 'I have to lose my ambition for an ambitious painting to come up...the best ones are never by me, they don't belong to me, they just passed by.'

The eldest son in the village is obliged to carry the burden of patrimony. The younger is freer. He is on threshold of staying or leaving. Before the war migration agents came to the villages to lure people to America. Those who had little prospects of an inheritance and a strong drive left.

Yves was neither bound by these codes, nor enticed to travel to his mother's homeland. He was not dazzled by the lustre of the art world. His feet were rooted in Quincy. None of his friends spoke of leaving. The boys from Ley were happy to continue their fathers' businesses as builders of chalets. The growth in tourism made the valley thrive. They eventually bought good cars, always wore fashionable clothes, and had lovely parties.

8. Free Radical Photographs and the Frustrated Actor

The first Christmas I spent with John and his family was in 1994. John had rushed to get back to Quincy from Paris. I flew over from Manchester. John's gift to me was a copy of *Pages of the Wound*. It was a collection of poems and photographs that were hand-printed by John Christie. In the late 1950s John met Anya Bostock. She was of Eastern European descent, but was born in Harbin, China. After graduating from Oxford, she reviewed for the *Manchester Guardian* and translated classic texts from German and Russian. In the first summer that John met Anya he also learned photography. *Pages of the Wound* includes his black-and-white photos of the curves from her shoulder to her hips. Her body flows in the long grass of the Alpes-Maritimes. These images evoke those long amorous afternoons when the sun conspires with the lover's bliss. In such moments, even though the shadows are getting longer it is as if the sun has forgotten to set.

John was drawn to the camera as a means to explore intimacy.

At the same time Susan Sontag had launched her polemic text *On Photography*. She challenged the way photographers both ripped images from their context and fed perverted fantasies. She showed how the camera was instrumental in decontextualising history and commodifying subjects. It was a weapon for surveillance and fuel for pornography. It created a picture of the world that was, in her words, 'reduced to a series of unrelated, free-standing particles'.

John never disputed these tendencies, but he hung on to the redemptive uses of photography. For him, it had the potential to do something more – to be a connector between different contexts, to redeem experience, and to serve as a memento of a life being lived.

In a television interview with Susan Sontag in 1983, he faces her across a wide table. Sontag is upright, fierce and precise. John is constantly leaning over the edge of the table trying to get closer to her.

His hands are busy fumbling for words. As he bends forward it is as if he is attempting to smuggle in something that an interview between experts is meant to forbid – doubt and play. Sontag will have none of it! She is imperious, and indomitable.

John learned much more from his friend Jean Mohr. They complemented each other. John had a restless energy and Jean was a subtle force. Jean's father was a German who migrated to Geneva, and when Hitler came to power he applied for Swiss citizenship. Jean was born Hans-Adolf but his parents, who were anti-Nazis, changed it in 1939. Jean studied economics and became a photographer in his thirties. He worked for the International Red Cross and United Nations High Commission for Refugees. Humility was a feature that both Jean and John shared. However, Jean had a deeper sense of patience. He would say that when a subject had enthralled and wrapped its power over him, he would wait and let it settle. They collaborated in many books: *A Fortunate Man* (1967), *Art and Revolution* (1969), *A Seventh Man* (1975), *Another Way of Telling* (1982), *At the Edge of the World* (1999), *Derrière le miroir* (2000), *100 Photographs by Jean Mohr for the Freedom of the Press* (2010), and *John by Jean* (2016).

It rains a lot in the Alps. Even in the summer. This can delay the haymaking, and even worse if the rain continues for more than a day or two, it can ruin the freshly cut grass – the nutrients rot, rendering it into bland straw. During such pauses Yves and John would draw. Sometimes I would model for them. Or else I would go and chop wood. I loved the feeling of a heavy axe falling into the sweet centre of a log and then seeing the chips fly into the air. Just as I was completing one such mighty swing a small white car turned the corner of the barn and pulled up right beside me. The large chip of wood gracefully arced over the open rooftop, gliding past the smiling face of the driver, and then landed with a gentle thud on the damp verge. It was all in slow motion, and I was horrified, but the driver, Jean Mohr, seemed unperturbed.

Jean lived in Geneva. He had come over for coffee. John was thrilled to see him. He could not stop talking and showing him different things all afternoon. Jean nodded. Sipped his drink. Smoked a few cigarettes. He was tall and lithe. Quiet, unassuming but he also possessed an unflappable firmness. His left shoulder tilted a bit and there was a slight groove forged by the straps of his heavy equipment.

Jean was the perfect observer. He was introverted and modest. His gaze always appeared to be distracted even when he was staring. Meticulous and punctual, he also had the casual stance of someone who did not mind the fact that a close-up lens was missing. He kept his actions to a minimum. His camera was always visible, but he never seemed to be using it.

John was more of the extrovert when they were together. On other occasions he would prefer to be the listener. He would prefer the freedom of allowing his attention to wander – to pause on the hook of the teapot spout, to lose itself in the fold of the curtains. Designs were prompts to ruminate on the order of things. In these contemplative moments questions came later. Their arrival could be seen in the quiver of his lips and the shuffling of his feet. When Jean visited, John assumed a different role. He was part court jester, part newsreader.

It was delightful seeing John putting on such a performance. In sync, Jean and John butt out their cigarettes in the round glass ashtray. John crunches his down and little flashes of flaming tobacco sparkle. Jean slowly lowers his into the tray after the mute smoke had already vanished.

The following weekend Jean returned with a batch of photographs. There were countless images of John – his eyes sparkling, his smile and stubble glistening. I was sitting at the same table when all these photographs were taken. There were even photos of John and me, as well as my BMW Boxer and his Honda Blackbird. I don't recall seeing Jean pointing his camera at us. If he did, it must have been between breaths.

On more than one occasion the people in Jean's photographs turned to him and commanded attention. A generation later, this switching of agency, and in general, the development of a more collaborative approach to photography was to become more prominent. For instance, Paz Errázuriz, the Chilean photographer who documented the lives and loves of inmates in a mental asylum, was told by one couple that the photograph she took on their behalf was like a 'wedding certificate'.

We say that when we fall in love we are madly in love. To be registered insane is to lose the right to both plunge into and own love.

In Germany, while Jean and John were observing the conditions of the *Gastarbeiter*, a Turkish man jumped from the factory floor and onto a platform. He thrust his arms out in the starfish pose. His moustache burst its banks: 'Me, don't I exist, am I a nothing?'

Jean had taken many portraits that day. He was now summoned to take one more.

One of the central figures in *Another Way of Telling* is a peasant called Marcel Nicoud. Jean photographed him: tending to his cows, walking with his grandson up steep fields, preparing food in his dark kitchen. Marcel was wealthy in comparison to the other peasants in the village – he had fifty cows – but he worked just as hard. In one striking image he was wearing a buttoned-up fine-knit sweater. He was freshly shaved, and his hair was neatly parted. His hands were resting firmly against his hips, and he has declared to Jean that this is how he wants his grandson to remember him.

August Sander was the son of a carpenter working in the mining industry. In 1914 he photographed a group of young peasants dressed in dark suits, white shirts, ties and hats. The photograph is titled 'Three Farmers on Their Way to a Dance'. John's essay 'The Suit and the Photograph' (1980), which focuses on this image, is visceral. He contrasts their appearance with that of a group of elderly bourgeois men. On the peasant's body the sleeves are a bit too long and the cuffs on the trousers are baggy and dragging. They are wearing clothes they cannot afford and standing on the edge of a muddy field. The bourgeois are inside their stuffy and overly cushioned office. The older men are bald and spectacled. The hands of the peasants are coarse and ironically holding canes that, like Charlie Chaplin, they don't really need to lean on. The peasants are all wearing shoes that don't match their suits.

My father's toes were scrunched together. I assumed that this was from the pointy-toed shoes that were fashionable in the 1960s. My mother scoffed: 'In his village they all wore pigskin *tsarouchia* or wooden clogs – even to bed!'

John's hands were also rough. He had no fear of putting them into the dirt and using them as tools. Even after his long showers the cracks in his fingers and thumbs were embedded with earth. Seeing these little black lines in his fingers, as he waved them like a conductor searching for the right words, was a reminder that the seasons leave their mark and that thoughts can also come from the soil.

The oldest photo I have of my father was the one taken when he did his military service. It is the size of a passport photo. When he arrived in Australia he posed regularly. Always in a dark suit, white shirt and narrow tie. There is even one in which he is standing before the Exhibition Building, with its famous dome that is exactly one square metre bigger than Saint Paul's in London. He is holding a briefcase that he probably borrowed from the photographer. The proud smile is like the one of a young man who rents a sports car. The briefcase confused me when I was growing up. Was there another career between peasant, soldier, factory worker and taxi driver?

Jean Mohr took a loving image of Marcel Nicoud embracing his grandson. The ease and comfort in each other's arms were palpable. The little boy's eyes are hungry to do everything. Jumping before learning. Marcel probably hugged him more than he ever did his own son.

John's first grandchild was Chloe. From the card that Orestis and Katya sent I could sense that they were not only thrilled to be parents but delighted in their gift to John. For Christmas John bought Chloe an electronic talking parrot. We all loved it. Yves said that the parrot spoke better French than I did. Katya was not amused. She did not like the idea that her daughter would learn from a parrot. She gave a stern look of disapproval. The following year Chloe got a stuffed marmot. Still Katya did not approve. I never saw John's other son Jacob at these gatherings.

One evening Yves suggested that we should go to the restaurant that was higher up the mountain – at Sommand. It specialised in serving thin slices of beef that were grilled on the hot granite stone that was sunk in the middle of the table. As we parked John noticed that Marcel's old barn door was open. The barn was pristine. The grandson was back from his studies at university. The sparkle in the eyes that Jean Mohr captured almost twenty years earlier was still luminous. John invited him to the restaurant.

'First, I must deliver this baby calf, then I will clean up and join you.'

'Ah,' said John. 'Do you need any help?'

'No. It is all normal and everything should be easy.'

He had done these deliveries many times before with his grandfather. His hands moved with calmness and precision. We watched. He seemed to be proud of his role, and with us as witnesses he was even a bit cocky. But he preferred to complete the task alone.

John grunted his assent. I took a step back towards the door of the barn, but my eyes never left the scene.

The cow lowed, arched her back, and raised her tail. Marcel's grandson plunged his arm into the cow and searched for the calf's haunches. As the hooves protruded, he tied a rope and tugged to initiate the passage – it was a smooth, normal, miraculous liberation. The baby calf came into this world with a jump start – the mucus drooped, and tiny rivulets of blood dripped. The pounding of its heart was visible through the glistening coat. The mother leant over and licked the calf's face. The calf wobbled in a drunken stance and sniffed hungrily. The breath of the birth filled the barn. Outside the night sky was in majestic harmony. The stars seemed to lean closer – almost touching the roof of the barn.

'What do you mean he doesn't have a mobile?'

'He doesn't have a mobile phone,' repeated Orestis.

'But we want to invite him to open an exhibition.'

'Send him a fax.'

Giving up, but also having second thoughts, the Greek museum director muttered: '*C'est impossible!*'

Yes, there was a fax machine at Quincy. However, every time there was a lightning storm it would blow out. That would mean a trip out to Taninges where there was a Mr. Bricolage megastore. Thank God Lévi-Strauss did not live to see his term for the intelligence of assemblage being used as the brand name for the *supermarché*! John was allergic to malls. He would walk past the neon-lit display of meats and throw his hands in the air: '*Regard, regard.* It looks like a traffic accident.' For John malls and motorways were on the same spectrum as the penitentiary. Inside these zones everyone is a prisoner – an anaesthetised zombie.

By contrast, buying meat in Mieussy was like having an appointment with a Zen master. Bauge was a giant of a man, but he wore tweed jackets with a coarse weave and the daintiest little pink cravats.

Upon entering the butcher shop all you could smell was his brusque cologne. The display was pristine. Amidst red beef and pink veal there were rows of herbs. Not a single drop of blood anywhere. For each cut of meat, he had a special knife. The blade would enter from its tip, gliding between tendons and bone. There was little sign of strain on his huge hands and the force on the blade was subtle. As he wrapped the steaks in waxed paper, he would raise his eyes over the last fold: 'Not more than five minutes on high heat.'

John would nod in vigorous agreement. He was also bowing in reverence to the uneven balance between human and animal sacrifice. There was no hint of a vegetarian sentiment, but to waste food was criminal. As we left another customer would enter. Discreetly.

Most phone calls with John were usually treated as a kind of military operation. Information and instructions were exchanged with a brisk pace. In the evenings friends like the Brahmin poet Victor Anant would ring for a chat. We knew it was Victor because of the alternating nicknames and fake addresses.

'Hullo Monkey. Donkey calling from La Coruña, Spain.'

'Hullo Donkey. Monkey receiving in Hamburg, Germany.'

'Monkey, stop shooting with your tail!'

They would tease each other, and John filled the kitchen with rhythmic chuckles.

John had no time for gossip either on the phone or in any conversation. However, he never held back during controversies. During the 'Rushdie Affair', he did not privilege the liberty of the author over indignity towards the faithful. He supported the article that condemned Salman Rushdie that prompted Edward Said to resign from the board of *Race and Class*. He also loved predictions. He would be enthralled if anyone could spot a new trend and match it with a character type, such as Thatcher and Thatcherism. Add a use-by date in the conclusion and he would slap his knee and leap to exclaim: 'You're right. You're right!'

His own writing combined the pithiness of journalism with a flourish of sage prophecy. 'For the first time... Never again will we see... The greatest painter of his time... ' Art historians hated these definitive claims, but young students loved them. When he spoke in the kitchen about the future he tended to whisper, and his statements were released in hushed tones. Until he delivered his final point.

'I give it six months maximum. Then John Major will bring it all down like a house of cards.'

His hands would make a short sharp sweeping gesture, like a horizontal guillotine.

John's great love and deepest frustration was the cinema. He was in awe of Tarkovsky's films and adored the actor Tilda Swinton. Since the 1960s John had made countless documentaries for television. In the 1970s he wrote three screenplays for the Swiss director Alain Tanner. In his collaboration with Tanner, he felt his role was over once the script was delivered. He did not see how he could help in the filming. He kept his distance because he believed that any further interpretation would either confuse the actors or dilute the role of the director.

Working with the filmmaker Tim Neat was different. With a tiny budget in 1988 they made *Play Me Something*. The film was set in an airport terminal in the Scottish Hebrides. A group of strangers are waiting for their flight. An enigmatic figure appears and enchants them with a story of an Italian in Venice. John played the role of storyteller. It received an award that included partial funding for a follow-up film. John dreamed of being an actor. He could mesmerise an audience when he told stories or delivered lectures. However, the physical act of slipping into the form of another person was not a smooth step for him. Actors, like his friend Tilda Swinton, seem to have that capacity to lose themselves in their roles, or at least to show very little of their own consciousness. John's intellectual presence was heavy on his shoulders.

In 1990 John and Tim Neat began, and three years later eventually completed, the film *Walk Me Home*. Nella insisted that he take lessons. He worked so hard. She co-wrote the script and he played the part of William who was reflecting on the ideological collapse of the Soviet Union and the restructuring of the economy in the West. Both films are love stories about how an older man and a younger woman can refresh each other's perspective on life.

Like most people of their generation John and Beverly had that disgusting habit of smoking. I was repulsed by chain-smokers – they seemed to be slaves to their addiction. Mercifully he was not a heavy smoker. In fact, he maintained a rather dignified manner of only smoking either after dinner, or when in good company and in a café. He selected his time with cigarettes, a deliberate act of celebration or an accompaniment that offered comfort from the weather. In such instances I found delight at his pleasure. The strike of the match sparked joy and the conscious exhaling of smoke suspended time. I even enjoyed the twirling of the cigarette stick in his fingers. In Mieussy I bought a Zippo lighter from the *tabac*. In a single gesture I could flick the lid and roll the flint wheel over my jeans.

However, there was no sign of the joy in savouring the smoke when he was stressed. Instead, he would reach into the cupboard where Beverly kept her stash of cigarettes and suck on them with short sharp fierce motions. Butting out the stubs even though a third of the cigarette was still dangling.

The long phone calls with Tim Neat about reshoots and finances drove him to despair. After *Walk Me Home* was shown at the Edinburgh International Film Festival it was withdrawn by the producers, so that it could be reworked. It has never resurfaced. Tim kept a 35 mm print under his bed. He was more philosophical about this state of limbo. Geoff Dyer, a close friend but serious critic, called the film a 'balls up'. What made John fume were the endless delays, distractions and prevarications by the producers. The lisp and stammer that he probably got at boarding school came wobbling back. He would writhe, shout and pull his hair. At the end of such tiresome calls, it was as if Zeus had thrown a lightning bolt through the phone.

9. An Elegy for Leaving

When Susan Sontag visited Roland Barthes, she was disappointed by the size of his library. She could see all the books he had written about. But not much more. Surveying the shelves, she concluded that it was not a comprehensive collection. Or maybe Barthes only kept the books he read that he thought were worth writing about. If Susan dared to visit John in the village, she would have been even more disappointed. His library included Martin Heidegger's *Being and Time*, Ernst Gombrich's *The Image and the Eye*, as well as novels by friends such as Michael Ondaatje and Anne Michaels. They stood on the shelves like the beacons by which he navigated his journeys. However, he did not have a library.

The short essay on the stranger by the German philosopher Georg Simmel was very influential to me. It was written at the beginning of the twentieth century. Simmel came from an assimilated Jewish family. He witnessed a massive migration to the metropolis and suffered the stigma of anti-Semitism. With stunning perspicacity, he articulated the stranger's capacity to oscillate between different worldviews and form judgements through comparative thinking. Simmel was also an inspiration for the Polish-British sociologist Zygmunt Bauman. My interpretation of the role and perspective of the stranger in John's writing was heavily in debt to both sources. I wanted Zygmunt Bauman to be the examiner of my PhD but my supervisor Tony Giddens, who was also his publisher, thought that he was too prickly. I got the mellifluous Stuart Hall instead. When I met Zygmunt in Manchester and offered him a copy of my book on John, he thanked me and informed me that he had already read it when he examined my dissertation. 'Not possible,' I thought to myself. He may have been one of the readers for my book proposal. John and I talked a lot about Bauman's writing. Over the years a few of Bauman's books moved from his desk in the upstairs bedroom to the kitchen table. The kitchen was John's favourite room in the house.

After his retirement as head of sociology at Leeds University Zygmunt wrote over a dozen books on the 'liquid' forms of modernity. They resonated with John's views on estrangement. They shared a common indignation against the senseless flows of capital and its evisceration of traditions. If you look close enough you can hear echoes of Bauman in the later essays by John, but also you can see a continuous line in John's writing that unfolds, one way, and then another, from before, and after Bauman. The same zigzagging process of confirmation and elucidation can be traced in his relationships to Walter Benjamin, Roland Barthes, Georg Lukács and Gilles Deleuze. When he arrived at each of these authors, it was as if the other beacons in his library had already directed him to this destination. Benjamin was the guiding angel in *Ways of Seeing*. Barthes showed how a redemptive voice was the way to open a new vista into the meaning of photography. Lukács was an enduring presence on art and politics, and later on John saw how Deleuze could help to unfold the role of imagination. Hence, the feeling of déjà vu is a confirmation, even when it is an extension into something new.

I never saw my father read a book. He would rather play backgammon than go to the theatre. And yet, the articulation of his values – the duty of hospitality, the need for independence – were Homeric and Socratic to the bones. He was taciturn and tolerant, but some lines could not be crossed, and if they were, he would explode in rage. In 1971 my father was waiting at the bank in Kastoria. He had sold our house in South Melbourne and had gone back to Greece to explore the option of repatriating the family. The junta was still in power. A black-shirted fascist jumped the queue. My father pushed him back in place. The fascist growled.

'Don't you know who I am?!'

My father took a step closer to his face.

'I don't care who you are. I am an Australian and in Australia people don't push in.'

When he got to the counter, he emptied out his account and said to himself: 'This is no place for my children.'

He re-emigrated to Australia.

John had arrived in the village when the era of mass European migration from country to the city was almost over. When John walked to Louis's house, he did so slowly with his hands clasped behind his back. He was delighted when neighbours visited and was at ease with himself in the markets. Whenever we drove into Geneva, he was irritable, agitated and sarcastic. He couldn't get out of there quick enough.

When my grandfather was born the border between Greece and the Ottoman Empire was a few hundred miles south of his village. In those times peasants were still the vast majority in Europe. Now they are few, old and exotic. In my lifetime there has been an epochal shift. What has been abandoned by the seductions of city life? I could condense this list by noting the *scope* of our gaze, rhythms and wagers! What is the horizon before us in the city? Do we feel the cosmos weaving the seasons of our work? When we gamble, chance our arm, take a risk – what are we up against? For John, the sight of the migrant struggling in the city and the hope of renewal was always tinged with the pathos of the loss of traditional life. The 'we' in the peasant got weaker.

After the French Revolution in 1789 the next great event in Europe was the Greek Revolution in 1821. The theatre of the French Revolution was in the cities. Greeks found the road to freedom through the countryside. Modern Athens and Sparta had been long reduced to small inconsequential towns.

The story of the Greek Revolution is rightly told as a heroic battle for independence. This was the first country in Europe to successfully throw off the imperial yoke. The Greeks were surrounded by empires on land and sea.

Where did the audacity to demand freedom and autonomy come from?

To this day historians answer this question by pointing to the inspiration of Enlightenment ideals, the political manoeuvrings of the Greek diaspora, and the influence of philhellenes. There is no doubt that without the ideological groundswell, the supply of funds and guns, as well as the goodwill from the enemies of the Turks, the Revolution would have been delayed. Byron was a wonderful poet and very good in bed, but he was useless on the battlefield. Nothing would have been won without the fierce determination, and cunning calculation of the doggedly idealistic peasants. The winners – the educated Greek elites – used quotes from antiquity, imported a king from Bavaria, rebuilt civic institutions with sumptuous neoclassical architecture, and quickly proceeded to 'cleanse' the language so that the peasants could not administer their own lives.

The peasants told each other different stories. Yiannis Makriyannis, a brilliant and illiterate general, was desperate to tell the story from his perspective. In church the peasants understood very little, but they all admired the icons. Makriyannis summoned painters who had been trained in Paris and Vienna. Seeing their preparatory sketches, he recoiled. He then turned to Panagiotis Zographos, a fighter and naïve folk artist from the village of Vordonia. Together, they revisited the famous battle scenes. Zographos used multi-perspectival close-ups and broad vistas to capture what Makriyannis described as the spirit of being in the 'we not the I'.

Everyone else, revolutionaries such as Marx, ignored the dreams and defiance of the peasants. The subalterns were not meant to speak up.

John's trilogy *Into Their Labours* is a very late but great testament to this secret perdurance. My father was not alone in his defiance. His brother and sister joined the Communist *andartes*/partisans in the Second World War and fought in the ensuing civil wars. It was his great-grandfather that had the audacity to be free. As Teodor reminded John in the documentary on *Pig Earth*, it was also the peasants in Russia, China, Cuba, Vietnam that won the wars of liberation.

Revolutionaries relied on peasants but only Gramsci understood that their conservative mindset was not purely reactionary. He recognised that the peasant's scepticism was different to the ruling class's wish to preserve the status quo. The peasants dreamed of a better life, one that was unencumbered by hardship and exploitation. They were also wary of shaded promises and cautious until an alternative could be fully proven. They hung on to their optimism like a fragile relic. John insisted that the peasants were not rigid thinkers that were stuck in their ways – they were alert witnesses and keen observers. Their hands were quick to probe and test for more ingenious ways to complete a task. However, he also admired their silent resistance to the grand promise of progress. Revolutionaries wanted the world to believe in a giant leap forward, the peasant responded, first show me a small step. They did not think that life could be guaranteed. They knew from the wider horizon of experience that it was capricious. In that sense, our older pagan ways were more honest, and in such gods we can still believe.

The State Library in Melbourne, like the one in Manchester, is modelled on the British Museum Reading Room in London. Of course, the dome in Melbourne is bigger and brighter. I would study there as an undergraduate. In 1983, after a lecture on 'Art and Politics' by Don

Miller, I found a recent copy of *Aspect*, a journal on art criticism. It was lying on the desk, and inside was an interview between John and the Australian political scientist Humphrey McQueen. In response to the opening question on the influence of his teachers at art school, John stressed the vitality of proposing a position: a line that the student can either follow or oppose.

> Because every tradition has broken down, students are presented with the work from half-a-dozen civilisations and then told to get on with it. Various teachers can pass on various methods or demonstrate their own personal ad hoc solutions, but very seldom is any consistent line of purpose or development established in a school. As a result, students can neither conform, nor rebel. The majority simply flounder, and their flounderings are called 'experiments'.[4]

A decade later, while I was teaching in the sociology department at the University of Manchester, my friend Pavel Büchler offered me a job teaching critical theory in the new Master of Fine Arts at the Glasgow School of Art. Pavel was a Czech refugee with no formal qualifications. He was a brilliant thinker on the history of photography, an incurable raconteur, and the gold-medal winner in all jokeathons. Before my arrival he announced his decision to the students. They were not impressed and demanded the right to consultation. Pavel lit another Gitane and waited. They talked and consensus was formed. A tall Canadian stood up and announced that they would like to be taught by Theodor Wiesengrund Adorno.

Pavel didn't blink. 'Adorno is dead, so you will get Papastergiadis.'

I did my best to keep a straight face. I don't know how Pavel introduced me to his colleagues behind my back, but in that year, there were almost as many staff members attending my seminars as there were students.

There was no direct train from Manchester to Glasgow and so I would change at Preston Station. No sooner had I alighted from the local train than I realised that my brand-new cashmere scarf was left behind on the seat.

As I crossed the footbridge to get to the other platform, I noticed a lost-and-found depot. There was no queue, thirty minutes to kill, so I thought to myself why not fill in a form. The lady at the desk was also very sympathetic.

A short distance into my next train ride, an announcement came over the speakers.

'Will Mista Paapa...sterrr...giaaaaa...dis make himself known to the conductor as he walks through the carriages.'

As the tall burly conductor in a navy-blue uniform and silly hat with thin red stripes appeared, I put up my hand, not knowing if I was in trouble or not.

'Did you lose something on your last train ride?'

'Yes, a grey scarf.'

'Is this it?'

The sympathetic lady at the Preston lost-and-found depot rang the conductor on my previous train. He picked up my scarf and handed it to a guard at the next station. She had also figured out that the two trains briefly share part of their journey in the Lake District. The train I was now travelling on had slowed down as we approached the station, and the guard was poised to relay my scarf to the next conductor.

This was the same scarf that I subsequently wrapped around John's neck as we walked out of the theatre on a cold winter's night in London. John snorted and cuddled into it with gratitude. The scarf was still warm from my body. He accepted it like a soldier taking a cigarette from his friend. The scarf left my hand. He let it dangle around his open neck. Simon McBurney had performed in and directed Ionesco's

The Chairs. We went to a bar and listened to stories by the enigmatic designers Brothers Quay. John nodded approval to most things that night but barely said anything.

Did London, like Paris, and any other imperial capital, make him taciturn?

The first time I saw John in London I was in the lecture theatre at the British Film Institute. John gave a brief lecture on cinema and then did a Q&A with Colin McCabe. He was spotlit and that just emphasised the extent to which he was writhing and squirming in that darkened space. He only gathered his breath the moment he paused to pick up the faux doily, which was under his glass, and reflected on the intelligence of folk patterns. In the foyer he finally began to smile. He had ridden over from Paris with Nella as his pillion. She was still in her leathers and in full command of the bar. He was happy to lean into the glow around her shoulders.

The other occasions were also riven with nerves. His novel *To the Wedding* was dedicated to the victims of AIDS. He came to do a reading at the London Lighthouse – a hospice for AIDS patients. Royalties from the novel are still directed to this benevolent organisation. The death of Christina, his Spanish daughter-in-law, was still raw in him. She was Jacob's partner. I met Jacob once and he spoke to me about John in an abstract and intellectual manner. Jacob is a filmmaker. John gave me the impression that he and Jacob clashed on most things. In 2002 Jacob made a film starring Gérard and Guillaume Depardieu which was bizarrely called *A Loving Father*. It tells the story of a son who kidnaps his father, who is on his way to Sweden to collect a Nobel Prize. While the father is held hostage the son attempts an awkward reconciliation and then proceeds to go to Stockholm to accept the prize on behalf of his 'loving father'. The film is a cringing testament to an unresolved relationship. Jacob and Katya grew up in Geneva with Anya. Katya has John's laser focus and convictions. She is sharp and clear in her judgements but also quick to laugh and show kindness. She adored her father. Jacob worked in the same field as John, but it was as if he resented the shadows that were cast by his father.

The following night John and I agreed to stage one of our 'kitchen conversations' at the Institute of Contemporary Art. I was a regular speaker at that venue. He did not want to do the usual chitchat: 'Tell us more about your influences' and 'How did this character come to you?' I knew that this would be excruciating for John, but perhaps I over-prepared in the opposite direction. It was a disaster. When we arrived in the Carlton Room it was as if we were suddenly transformed into aliens that were approaching each other from different planets. Awkward silences and weird tangents. He seemed to be elsewhere.

When John did interviews on television his gaze locked onto the eyes of the interviewer. In an amphitheatre with hundreds of other eyes it was different. The tide pulled him out and away from his partner. I noticed this when he spoke with the Welsh poet Gareth Evans. Once again, he struggled to sit still. He was desperate to join with the crowd. After our conversation at the ICA we had dinner with Piotr Anderszewski, a Polish concert pianist. He was even more anguished about his impending performances. A few years earlier Piotr had come to attention when, after stumbling on a single note, he walked out of his performance in the finals of a competition in Leeds. He was an unbending purist and would often repeat an entire recital if he felt he got one tiny part wrong. John encouraged Piotr, and this was a sort of consolation to me. As I left, we hugged, he kissed his palm and stroked the protruding cylinders on my BMW Boxer.

John had a soft spot for Poles. They had endured all the extremes of political domination and had become resistant to the 'power-shit' of institutional promises. In his neighbourhood in Paris there were many Polish migrants who were experts at fixing faulty lights and getting around obstacles. They told mischievous stories, had deep memories, and they knew where to find wild sorrel. John loved sorrel soup. The Poles also had a habit of looking a little sad even when they were happy.

In Glasgow I conducted studio visits in the semi-derelict old Girls' High School. The students were not short of space, and they used every media imaginable. Welding components from store fridges, splicing sadistic 'happy slapping' videos, embroidering quotes from Baudrillard, photographing pure white Icelandic landscapes. Where does an interlocutor begin?

Jochen Gerz, an artist famous for his interventions in public spaces and an ex-boxing journalist, had a golden rule in his studio visits. The first meeting was always after lunch, and the first question was:

'What problem have you been working on this morning?'

The students would often slip into their well-rehearsed script on the conceptual meaning of their practice. Jochen would interrupt.

'We will get to the big picture later. Let us begin with concrete details. What is the specific task that you have set for yourself today?'

Zoom in to the particular and it will also reveal the cosmos. It is not easy, but it is necessary to find a simple structure if you want to convey complex ideas. And vice versa.

Different thinkers have shaped John's thought throughout his life. He acknowledged that Walter Benjamin was a major influence for *Ways of Seeing*. Georg Lukács was the imaginary interlocutor for *G*. The Marxist art historians Frederick Antal, Max Raphael and Ernst Fischer were models from the beginning of his art writing and peaked in his book *The Success and Failure of Picasso*.

One summer a book by Simone Weil, the lyrics of Tom Waits, and the looping track 'Jesus' Blood Never Failed Me Yet' by Gavin Bryars were everywhere in the Quincy kitchen. John had an old cassette recorder, and we would listen to Bryars with a coffee in hand. I was also drawn to the ambient music of Brian Eno, as well as Steve Reich. I felt close to this music. It had an affinity with *moirologia*, the Greek laments for the dead. The subtle process of variation had an uplifting effect on me. The movement kept returning to an original motif, but it also headed elsewhere. Ernst Bloch described Bach's fugues as an aesthetic of equanimity. They were expressive of an interregnum – a time when the *ancien régime* was dying and the new rulers had not yet found their strut. Minimalist music also conveyed my sense of being suspended. I knew that I had lost touch with the peasant heritage of my parents, but I was not comfortable in the suburban skin of disco music and the purchase of a sports car for the son attending university as a sign that the family had made it.

I asked John how he would describe this contemporary music. He said: 'Elegiac.'

Such music filled me. I could feel sad without collapsing into hopelessness. In fact, what I felt most was the hope rising out of the sadness. The sounds drifted along a long plateau that was neither flat, nor depressing. I told John about the pirate radio stations run out of Moss Side in Manchester and a song called 'Home Is Where the Hatred Is'. He flinched. I showed him some images of the silhouettes by the Black American artist Kara Walker. He recoiled from the violence and was uncomfortable with the use of caricature.

John turned the conversation back to Gavin Bryars.

'Maybe it is more like a fugue.'

He stared out the window above the kitchen sink. The clouds were swirling. No chance the grass would dry today. Probably more rain and a good day for drawing in the studio.

He took a big sip of coffee and added.

'The tone of a fugue is of course sombre. It creates a kind of hollow, but inside that space there is a structure which is not formless. It has a movement which is subtle, and it tends towards a horizon rather than a point. The fugue speaks to us because it creates a sensation of sadness and hope without pinning a specific label on that feeling. Fugue evokes the feelings that occur before or somehow underneath those that are found in words like sadness.'

He then turned to the kitchen table and picked up a little French edition of a book by Simone Weil.

Simone Weil was a Catholic mystic, but John did not care about that. What attracted him was the clarity of her vision for justice, her conviction to expose the false distinctions between spirit and body, and the evanescent outlines of hope in all her words. At the time, we were deeply preoccupied by the horror of the war in Yugoslavia. John translated this passage for me. Later I found it in an English version.

> As for those who have been struck by one of those blows which leave a being struggling on the ground like a half-crushed worm, they have no words to express what is happening to them. Among the people they meet, those who have never had contact with affliction in its true sense can have no idea of what it is, even though they may have suffered a great deal. Affliction is something specific and impossible to describe in any other terms, like the sounds of which nothing can convey the slightest idea to anyone who is deaf and dumb. And as for those who have themselves been mutilated by affliction, they are in no state to help anyone at all, and they are almost incapable of even wishing to do so. Thus, compassion for the afflicted is an impossibility. When it is really found we have a more astounding miracle than walking on water, healing the sick, or even raising the dead.

I have returned to these words many times over the years. The meaning is obvious and ethereal, present and elusive. Like a message of boundless love which also miraculously rips open all the frontiers and thrusts the ego on waves that rise and fall, it draws you into a pulse that is both ancient and utopian and calls out a rhythm that can sweep everything from here to eternity.

John was interested in and gained an uncanny insight into many things. If you really wanted to insult him, you could say that he was a dilettante. But no dilettante sweated to achieve such precision and purpose. He did not see the world as a delicatessen filled with treats. There was for him the unending fight against injustice and the quest to tease out the hidden threads of hope. He turned to face the world with curiosity and a constant longing for a future homecoming. Looking at his work at any point, whether it is the beginning, middle or the end, there is both a development in the diversity and an 'astounding' miracle of continuity. John always said he saw fields. He searched for the flow of time extended across space. In the essay 'The Storyteller' he recounted a Russian proverb about walking across a field.

Experience is indivisible and continuous, at least within a single lifetime and perhaps over many lifetimes. I never have the impression that my experience is entirely my own, and it often seems to me that it preceded me. In any case experience folds upon itself, refers backwards and forwards to itself through the referents of hope and fear; and, by the use of metaphor, which is at the origin of language, it is continually comparing like with unlike, what is small with what is large, what is near with what is distant. And so the act of approaching a given moment of experience involves both a scrutiny (closeness) and the capacity to connect (distance). The movement of writing resembles that of a shuttle on a loom: repeatedly it approaches and withdraws, closes in and takes its distance. Unlike a shuttle, however, it is not fixed to a static frame. As the movement of writing repeats itself, its intimacy with the experience increases. Finally, if one is fortunate, meaning is the fruit of this intimacy.

Eugène Ionesco, the Romanian playwright, said that a writer is either writing a book or thinking about it. I never saw John cross-examining life and checking how it could fit in with his writing. The relationship between the events that surrounded him and the words he composed was palpable, but it was not linear. When he wrote the world encroached and occupied him – he surrendered and struggled. In lateral motions, through quotations and memories, it came in and out of his pages. However, when he was with us, chopping vegetables in the kitchen, or shopping at the market, it never felt that what was happening was a dress rehearsal for his work. Life has its own force and communing with its energy was not a walk in the park. In a letter he sent to me he said: 'Here is the manuscript. It is finished as am I.'

At the time I was writing my doctoral dissertation, postmodernism was frothing and throbbing in academia. I asked John what he thought of this concept. He looked slightly irritated by the question. Maybe it was the culmination of hay, dust and sweat that was stuck between his back and the blue singlet. Or it could have been that Yves was using up all the hot water in the shower. He took off his cap and smacked it against his knee.

'Nothing useful about freedom has come from it!'

Along the front of John's house was a bench – probably a pew from the village chapel. The postman left the mail there and the *Guardian Weekly* was always there to read when you were going to the outhouse. We sat in silence and waited for Yves to finish in the shower.

John was not anti-intellectual, but he was always impatient with academicism. He admired engaged scholars but also insisted on his independence from all institutions. On a train from Lucerne to Geneva he flicked through a thick catalogue that accompanied an exhibition by Degas.

'No help here,' he concluded.

His education on art, politics and ideas did not come from the university. He did go to the Chelsea Art School, but more importantly, it was a generation of postwar refugees who were his teachers. His first novel, *A Painter of Our Time*, recounts the struggles of a Hungarian artist Janos Lavin. The novel was inspired by the life of two Hungarians, his mentor Frederick Antal the art historian, and the artist Peter Peri.

Two of my professors took me further into John's writing. Don Miller lectured on art and politics. He introduced me to the collections of art essays *Permanent Red* and *Ways of Seeing*. Alan Davies, or Fu as he was reverentially referred to, said that he spent a year in London and would read John's weekly column in the *New Statesman*.

'A total education in art!'

Fu also alerted me to John's book *The Success and Failure of Picasso*. The book chronicled the failure of the French Communist Party to seize the opportunity of working with an artistic genius. Picasso said: 'Joining the Party was like a homecoming, but as in every family, there are some arseholes!'

Fu was more interested in the description of the partnership between Picasso and Braque in their pioneering days of cubist experimentation. John described them as two mountain climbers, tethered to each other, levering from each other, and thereby scaling an unknown precipice together.

'A brilliant metaphor for collaboration,' Fu trumpeted.

For those who were regular readers of John's newspaper and magazine columns, *Ways of Seeing* was not breaking news. The book distilled two decades of thinking on the role of art in revealing truth, the struggle of artists to outwit ruling-class worldviews, and the uses of new visual techniques to expand consciousness. John acknowledged that many of his ideas on the role of technology as a productive means to expand consciousness were derived from Walter Benjamin. In particular, he was in debt to Benjamin's essay 'The Work of Art in the Age of Mechanical Reproduction'. That essay was written in 1935 and first translated into English in 1969. Anya Bostock was a translator of many of the great German philosophers from the Frankfurt School.

Anya was also the cousin to the famous Australian medical scientist Gustav Nossal. I met Gus at a Christmas party hosted by Louise Neri in Melbourne. Gus was born to a Viennese Jewish family that had converted to Roman Catholicism. In 1939, fearing persecution from the Nazis, they migrated to Australia. After the war, Gus's family often returned to Europe. Gus told me of the wonderful lunches at Anya's apartment in Geneva and how he loved having Katya and Jacob bounce up and down on his knees. Many years earlier Katya told me about her uncle in Melbourne and how fondly she remembered bouncing on his knee.

Through Anya two streams converged in John's thought. She was the translator of many of the key texts from the Frankfurt School of critical theory, in particular the writing of Georg Lukács and, together with John they also translated Aimé Césaire and Bertolt Brecht. In the TV series of *Ways of Seeing* Anya also leads a feminist reading group that discusses the representations of the nude in art history. John's award-winning novel *G* is dedicated to Anya and 'her sisters in Women's Liberation'.

When John met Frederick Antal and Peter Peri, he was the same age as I was when I met him. He looked up to them in the same way that I looked up to him. To him Antal was the commanding general, and Peri was the artist that had already lived a revolutionary life. Acknowledging these men was not an admission of needing to live in someone else's shadow but a mark of gratitude. Other lives are not there to be copied, but they can be a guide. Am I who I am because of the connections and departures I made? We want to reach for unity by being close and then also strive for our integrity by leaving. For me in my late twenties and early thirties there was Rasheed Araeen, Teodor Shanin, Huw Beynon and Pavel Büchler. I worked side by side with them at the office of *Third Text* in London, the sociology department of Manchester University, and the Glasgow School of Art.

I learned a great deal from these men. Yet, I also felt that if I was ever to find my own form, then I would also have to go back to Melbourne. I put my passion into my work. This is a surplus that I wanted to control. I had learned much in the UK. I was inspired and encouraged by luminaries. I had come to the UK on a scholarship that was in part funded by the media mogul Kerry Packer. I did not feel a debt to him, but I wanted to be closer to the context in which my thinking on exile, migration and diaspora was formed. Most of the other young men who won the scholarship to Cambridge were scientists. They used the UK as a stepping stone to the big labs in the USA. I had zero interest in that country. I wanted my energy to oscillate between Europe and Australia. I had to find a way that combined these worlds. I did not want to remain an expatriate.

Teodor had recruited me to work with him at Manchester University and the Moscow School of Social and Economic Sciences. I watched him weep at the collapse of the Soviet Union and helped him build a school that would instigate a new transnational dialogue for the social sciences. In 1993 his mother called him from Tel Aviv. She was ill. He told her that he would abandon his trip to New York.

'No Teodor, you go, give your lecture, and on your way home, you come and see me!'

She died while he was in America. Teodor and his mother had fled Vilnius to escape the Nazis. He got scurvy in a Russian displacement centre. She found vitamin C pills sent by the Indian Communist Party to cure him. They moved across Europe and settled in Palestine. He fought in the liberation against the English occupiers. They were both disgusted by the Zionists. He became a world-famous professor who bridged Eastern and Western perspectives on the peasantry, and now, as he was making his way from the airport to her empty apartment, he was bereft and crushed by guilt.

I sat under the birch tree in his Fallowfield home and thought:

'I never want to receive that phone call.'

My father was a stranger to me for most of my life. He tended to defer to my mother. When I rang from England, he would usually be the first to pick up the phone.

'Are you okay sonny? Good. Talk to your mother.'

That was not a relationship. It was time to go back and play backgammon and listen. I returned after twelve years' absence. By then we had both become very different men. I was still striving and at times angry with the world. He had found his peace and satisfaction. His kindness blossomed. Everyone loved my father's smile. When he was dying his slow death with Parkinson's disease, Nuria, the Sudanese nurse, would lie beside him, feed him gently, comb his hair. As I walked in, she told me: 'I just want to share in the love that this man received and still gives.'

What did the end of the Soviet Union mean to John? I don't think it was a gaping wound. I could not discern any fresh cuts or scars. He was never a card-carrying member of any communist party. In fact, the Soviet ministers of culture had gone out of their way to scold him. He never doubted the validity of Marx's arguments, but he was also not convinced that it was a complete system.

John was both a romantic and a Marxist. He abhorred the trappings of institutional power. Dogma was just half-truths and stupidity in second-hand clothes. Hence, the collapse of the Soviet Union was shocking, but it did not derail him. His focus remained tied to the ground. The everyday struggles for love, compassion and solidarity. His eyes were both below and beyond the radar of the party system, and in that sense his commitments were bigger than the ideological version of politics. Like Oscar Wilde he found political meetings boring. He would choke waiting for his turn to pass a motion. He preferred being interrupted by a rude prick in the pub.

I belong to a generation of people who do not define their political allegiances in terms of specific parties. The party system had lost its grip on our imagination. Our vision of the world was muddled and confused. We were angry at injustice but did not agree with either the realism of the social democrats or the purity of the hard left. We were children when Che Guevara was killed. The victory of the Viet Cong was on distant black-and-white newsreels. The Russians were not superheroes, and everyone could tell that the East German swimmers were pumped with drugs. My father told me of how the Hungarian water polo team bloodied the pool when they faced off against the Soviet Union in the 1956 Melbourne Olympics. Hungary won 4–0. Days before Russian tanks had toppled their government. The collapse of the Soviet regime, which in one of its satellites had built a wall 'to keep out the capitalists', was neither a sign of change nor source of despair for us. We wanted to believe, we were too young to be cynical, but we were also not naïve.

When I was working in Moscow with Teodor, one of his most acerbic colleagues asked: 'Why do you come here?'

'To promote dialogue and equality.'

'You are silly. Can't you see. We are not Europeans. We are part Mongol. We like to smash things. First, we destroyed socialism. Now we will wreck capitalism.'

The village school came to the city. The Greeks in Melbourne were determined that their kids learned Greek. Anyone with the most rudimentary knowledge of grammar was recruited as a teacher. There was a myth in Greek history that under the Ottoman rule Greek schools were hidden in caves and lessons were taught by heroes in candlelight. Most of the Greek migrants in Melbourne were peasants. Few had progressed beyond primary school in the village. It was a rarity to meet someone who had gone to *gymnásio* – a higher school in a town.

At a community dance my father introduced me to a man who stared deep into my eyes. His suit and tie were more fashionable than my father's, but I could not see the point of the introduction. There was a long silence. Then my father added:

'He completed the *lycée*!'

I was ignorant that this was the intermediate qualification – between high school and university. In my teenage aloofness I smiled indifferently. I was glistening from dancing, feeling immortal, and unaware of the rarity of this level of education in our community. At those events, the music and food were usually rather ordinary. But everyone dressed like celebrities. There was a soccer player at a prominent table. He wore a beige suit with a satin shirt and an extra-wide tie. His girlfriend had a silk blue gown, an all-year-round tan and blonde hair. At that age I was impressed by the glamour of the soccer player, but I loathed my Greek teachers.

The Greeks settled in the inner suburbs of Melbourne. There were many empty parish halls and derelict churches. Even before the artists squatted in these vaulted spaces, and decades before the designers and developers had come to make their fortunes in gentrification, the Greeks had leased them as schools. The buildings were dusty and cold. In the corners or under the stages were trunks filled with prayer books, mouldy hymn sheets, moth-eaten tablecloths and a sweat-stained fencing suit. As kids our job was to set up the trestle tables, clean the old pews, and begin the class with a few star jumps.

My first teacher Kiria Efi lived in a two-storey Victorian terrace house just down the road from the school. She was kind and enthusiastic. Her toddler would sit in a cradle at the edge of the classroom. We sang songs and giggled a bit. I don't remember learning anything other than the alphabet.

The following year Kirio Dimitri arrived. He was young, stern, and slim. Additional classes were added. The hall was subdivided with partition walls. A blackboard was rolled in. Our new teacher had a steely gaze and never smiled. He always wore a black suit with stovepipe pants. He carried a metre-long stick. There was no need for him to use it because we were terrified. We sat silent as stones. Again, we learned nothing. We were too scared to turn our pages for fear of making a noise.

Classes were usually conducted on Tuesday and Thursday evenings. The other kids were playing on the wide streets lined with plane trees. We had to sit still in the freezing school.

One evening Kirio Dimitri missed class. The Head brought in Jim Karabatsos, who was the 'good' boy in the senior class. Jim was plump, walked in tiny strides, had memorised all the patriotic dates, and could recite poems about how much more the sun shone in Greece. Parents loved that these teachers were grinding nationalism into our bones. Jim was given Kirio Dimitri's stick and told to ensure that no noise came over the partition walls.

The Head walked away, and Jim immediately tested the stick on the top of the trestle table. The sound of the whack brought a lascivious smile onto his face. I was sitting next to my cousin Tassos. My parents owned a four-bedroom weatherboard house, and we were sharing it with his family. The Karabatsos family lived across the road in a two-toned brick-veneer home. In the same pew sat a pretty Aussie girl who had come to our school out of curiosity and to keep company with her Greek girlfriend. Jim could not take his eyes off her. He noticed that she was as rigid as the rest of us. At one point he called my cousin and me to the front.

'You were talking.'

'No, we weren't.'

'Open your hands.'

Whack! Whack!

We went back to our seats and whimpered like little dogs.

'Come back. I told you to be quiet.'

'But it hurts.'

'Open your hands.'

Whack! Whack!

This went on and on. The more he hit us the more intently the girl stared at Jim. It aroused him into a spiral of violence. By the time we got home our hands were so bruised and numb that we could not hold the spoon to eat our soup. Tassos's mother Marianthi was livid. She marched across the road and blasted the Karabatsos family. Mr Karabatsos did not work in factories like the other Greek men and women. He wore a tweed suit with a white shirt and sold the Encyclopaedia Britannica door to door. That night Aunt Marianthi brought him, and his stay-at-home wife, down.

The following Thursday Kirio Dimitri was back in charge. A tense silence was restored. We still learned nothing. At the end of the class Tassos's older brother Nick was waiting outside. He had never come to pick us up. We normally strolled home in the dark.

'Which one is he?'

'The one with the black coat buttoned up all the way to his double chin.' I said as I pointed to Jim Karabatsos.

'You and Tas run home.'

Nick walked up to Jim and thumped him straight in the nose. Then we all ran home laughing. Minutes later the Karabatsos family came to protest. Aunt Marianthi stood as wide as the door.

'What were all of you expecting?'

She spoke in the *plithintiko* – the formal plural to show that we might be peasants, but not dumb suckers.

If primary school Greek lessons were useless, then high school was not much better. We learned nothing but somehow, we all graduated with an A+. Mr Roubos taught mathematics at a technical college and ran a number of Greek schools which he had pretentiously named Pythagoras. For an extra fee he picked up and dropped off the kids in his blue-and-white Toyota minivan. His classes were on Saturday afternoons. I resented this even more because it clashed with my sporting events.

Kirio Dimitri walked around the classroom with a stick held behind his back. Mr Roubos would begin the class by removing the long black belt from his pleated pants. If he was in any way displeased it would come thrashing down on the table.

The Fascists in Greece would dispatch books to the diaspora. On the colophon page were two images: an owl framed by four letters – which we decoded as 'whoever reads is an idiot'; and the government symbol of a soldier standing upright in the flames of the phoenix. I must give it to the Fascists – they knew a thing or two about design and uniforms. Greek cinema also flourished in Melbourne.

On weekends the Astor Cinema in St Kilda and the Kinema in South Melbourne were packed. In between the screening of the comedy and the tragedy there was also a propaganda newsreel and then the weekly highlights of the soccer games. The Communists would throw their Coke bottles at the screen when the news came on. The cinema operators stopped showing the newsreel. The Fascists, who were cruel but not stupid, spliced the sport highlights into the newsreel. If the

Communists wanted to know if PAOK beat Olympiacos, then they would have to sit through the news.

I would find any excuse to miss Greek school. Rugby games at Geelong Grammar School. Cross-country races with Xavier College. Anything but Greek.

My brother Vasili was still in primary school, and he would have to make his way to the bus stop on his own. Towards the end of one class Mr Roubos threw a new textbook at him.

'Give this to your brother.'

The following week Mr Roubos asked me to present a summary of the first chapter.

'I didn't know that I was to be tested on the new book.'

Mr Roubos summoned my brother.

'Why didn't you tell him to do his lesson?'

My brother was quivering in fear. In a trembling voice he insisted that he was not given any instructions on a lesson. Mr Roubos was already raising his black belt and the gold buckle was shining bright.

'Open your hands.'

'If you are such a man, then hit me,' I interjected.

He didn't hesitate and whacked me on the hands and legs.

Kids in short pants, braying donkeys, liars with stupid grins on their faces, sullen mules, and dull bricks – it was all the same to him. Units.

That night I told my mother that Vasili and I were never going back to be one of the Pythagoras's asses. I swore to her that when I got my license, I would hunt down Mr Roubos and drive over him. She asked me to keep this from my father but that she would enrol us in the 'Academy' run by Mr Tsousis.

Mr Tsousis was gay and drove an Australian version of the luxury Cadillac. It was the first car I saw with air conditioning, and a radio with a cassette player. He was as much a showman as Liberace. However, he had already made a small fortune and was finally committed to delivering a decent education experience. He employed his nephew Mr Arsenakis – a kind and gentle young man who was studying architecture. Our classes were in a former Catholic school at the top of Richmond Hill. On our first day there was a total eclipse of the sun. We sat by the window which was elevated above our shoulders and tried to avoid the temptation of looking out. My father had driven us there in his new Silver Top Taxi.

'If he doesn't listen, then you can punish him,' he said to Mr Arsenakis while shaking his open palm.

Beatings and standing with one leg in the air was the way of his schooling in the village. How else can wild boys be tamed? My father always said a sapling needs a firm stake! Otherwise, we have chaos. Nikos Kazantzakis's father's instructions were the same: 'His bones are mine, his flesh is yours. Don't feel sorry for him. Thrash him and make a man of him.' Teachers had the right to flog the boys. My father did not believe that there was any other way. The child was still part beast and only a stick could straighten him out. He looked into the teacher's eyes to see if there was a conspiratorial exchange – like two hunters determined to root out their prey.

One of the worst curses to be heard from my father's mouth was the term *amorphote*. It meant you were uneducated and crude, but it also literally meant that you were without form. To be without form is to revert to the primal chaos from which the ordered cosmos emerged. Education was what raised us out of the formless. Without it we could not only fail to tame the beast within, but be nothing more than a blob, a void in the spectrum of humanity.

When we arrived at school my father paid the fees cash in advance. He abhorred debt more than a criminal avoids prison.

'How can you be free if you owe money to someone else?'

A peasant prefers a transparent exchange. They invest in their future by planting and storing in their barns. A loan should be minimal and exceptional, not a permanent and opaque part of conducting business. The Athenians believed a citizen was not free to participate in the polis if they were bonded to another in debt. My father taught me the pleasure of a purchase with money that was already in my hand rather than the credit that was promised by a bank.

When Karl Marx died the clerk at the registry office was in a quandary. He could see that Dr Marx was impoverished, but as he could not discern any previous form of employment, he entered 'gentleman' in the column for occupation. Marx's attitude towards the peasantry was not entirely wrong, but he was rather lazy and ignorant when he repeated the prejudice of his 'enlightened class'. The peasants did not have a monopoly on 'idiocy'. Engels, the heir to the factories in Manchester, was equally dismissive. He was convinced that industrialisation would spell the end of the peasantry as quickly as the 'steam engine smashes a wheelbarrow'. In the heady days of globalised market economies American presidents boasted that capitalism had lifted millions out of poverty. Less and less people lived side by side with their animals. However, inequality and insecurity, along with new forms of authoritarianism and surveillance were on the rise.

The eclipse was approaching and the sky outside the classroom window was getting darker. As my father was speaking, I could see my secondary school teacher Mr Arsenakis looking away. He knew where my father had come from. However, he still recoiled and looked out into the darkened afternoon skies. He did not accept my father's endorsement of violence, but he also said nothing. In that silence the gulf between me and my father deepened. I looked up at my father's gestures and my teacher's dismay and I could see myself disappearing into withdrawal. This was not the man I wanted to become. I would rebel by ignoring him. In fact, hadn't he already abdicated his authority with his nightly cheer – 'C'mon sonny, study, so that you don't grow up to be like me.'

Finally, with Mr Arsenakis we started to learn rather than monkey-mimic the propaganda. I sat with Angela Makris, the niece of Mr Tsousis, it was safe and delightful. I even enjoyed learning how to dance. Soon after, Mr Tsousis put me in the senior class. He taught us that the Marxists had different interpretations of Greek history. He didn't agree with all of it, but he insisted that it was important to listen to other perspectives.

In an interview for an arts TV program the Greek composer Manos Hadjidakis once said: 'To be an intellectual in Greece, you have to be either a communist, or a homosexual.'

He raised his left eyebrow, and with wry sweet adamance declared: 'I, for one, am *not* a communist.'

Dora, one of the voluptuous senior girls, encouraged me in debates and in dancing. Dora was blooming in confidence. I was tall so they put me in the front of the *syrtaki* circles. I tried to get in rhythm with the girls, but I still could not find a haircut that suited my thick curls, and my skin was bursting with pimples. The girls were in command, and I loved trying to follow their rocking and skipping steps. Suddenly, getting a tram to Greek school was exciting. I liked Mr Tsousis. When I finished high school, I asked him if he liked teaching.

'But of course! I love it. I am surrounded by young people, and they will keep me young forever.'

I imagined the PhD as a space for free thinking, but I discovered that it was treated as an initiation into 'disciplinary' thinking. My choice to work on John's books was driven by my hunger to find a link between the experience of migration and a critical view of the world. After he completed his masterpiece, *A Seventh Man*, he took a rear-view on his own preoccupations and recognised that 'all my writing is about emigration'. When we first met in Paris, he also saw that we shared a 'preoccupation with the nexus between exile and hospitality'. I am glad I started my career with John at my side, but the format of PhD was like a hostile terrain.

If I believed that there was some room for compromise in academia at the beginning of my career, I certainly think that there is even less now. The little zones of creativity and critical understanding have now been almost crushed by a culture of compliance. I work in a multicultural Australian university, but my head of school, dean, provos and vice chancellor are all recent English migrants. They are working hard to embrace our Indigenous history and ensure that the government's objective of ensuring the competence of the 'job-ready' next generation is achieved. My colleagues and I meekly grumble along hoping that every now and then something good can be sneaked into the room. We have become passive, and when we do make polite suggestions for change, we are informed that: 'Yes, there is a new committee that is looking into it.'

The relationship between leadership, research and teaching is now the inverse of what it was when I began my career. When I started, the most eminent scholars would accept a period as head or vice chancellor. They saw this role as a kind of civic duty. However, upon completing their term they were awarded a year-long sabbatical. In that way they returned to teaching refreshed and caught up with their research. This dutiful link between leadership, research and teaching has been broken. Twice I was approached by a head-hunter to take up a senior leadership role. I asked, how could I balance all my duties? The first time he replied: 'It will be difficult.' A few years later he knocked on my door again. I asked the same question. He replied: 'Now it is impossible to teach, research and lead. These jobs are for those who want to leave all that behind and move up the more lucrative management side of things.' It was a very short meeting. I was not prepared to snuff out the things I loved in my job, and feared becoming one of those cynics who is driven by resentment and opportunism.

John's house was ordinary. It was a typical peasant's house. The furnishings were basic. The book collection was modest, and there were only few artworks on display. There was not much evidence of his long history of involvement in art and politics. Yet, for me this simple home filled a void created as the other institutions were being eviscerated.

In 1987 Rasheed Araeen had established the journal *Third Text*. It opened a new path for engaging with artists beyond the Eurocentric paradigms. It was an incredible privilege to be invited to join his team. I worked with Rasheed and Jean Fisher for four years. I provided editorial assistance and was given the opportunity to edit a special issue: 'Auto-biography'. While I was in Quincy Rasheed sent me a fax. He wanted to pull in the focus on the special issue I was editing. I sat brooding under a tree in the garden. Reading and re-reading the page that smelled like tin. Rasheed complained that my approach was not suited for an art journal. I was neither an art historian nor an artist. My fantasy was that the journal could break out of not just the Eurocentric canon, but also academic divisions. *Third Text* was not just another space for non-Western artists, but also a space for mixing the visual and the literary, the philosophical and the political.

When I first joined the editorial team, I asked John to endorse the journal. He compared it to a 'skylight – one could look upwards through it: and one can read by it'.

For good and for bad, Rasheed always had the last word. When John saw my long face, he came and sat next to me in the shade.

'Nikos, you wanted this journal to be your home. It can accommodate some but not all of you.'

Rasheed always knew I could not stay there forever. We collided more than once. He made me chutney, cheese and ham rolls for lunch. He took the train to attend my graduation ceremony. And I looked at him with naïve incredulity when he told me parables about the Zen master's indifference at the departure of young monks.

My father had worked in factories and driven taxis for nearly fifty years in Australia. On retirement he announced with pride that he had enrolled in English classes for elderly migrants. Each night he did his homework and by morning he had forgotten almost everything. He laughed and rapped his knuckles on his 'cuckoo' head. His aim was to become competent enough to read the newspaper.

Midway through the term the school announced that it was closing. He loved his teacher and the warm feeling of being in a circle of students. He protested. The principal shrugged his shoulders and said something about a cost-benefit analysis. My brother felt sorry for our father and installed a satellite dish so that he could watch the Greek news channel.

'Have you heard about the fires near Sydney, sonny?'

'Yes Dad, they have been burning for over a week!'

'Oh, the Greek news on ERT has only just reported on them.'

'Are you going to vote with the Labor Party as always?'

'No, I vote Greens!'

'But Dad, you love chopping down trees, think planting concrete is a sign of progress, and you know that their leader Bob Brown is gay.'

'Better than all those other poofters, who sell everything and put refugees in prisons.'

Stuart Hall was one of the founding figures of the New Left and inventors of cultural studies. We met regularly at the advisory meetings for *Third Text*. At the opening of Okwui Enwezor's Documenta XI we had a coffee, and I recounted my father's sense of political alienation. He admitted sympathy but added another level to the dilemma.

'I feel the same. It is impossible to vote for the Labor Party, but it is also meaningless to vote for the Greens.'

My father might have felt abandoned by the Labor Party but was he really at home with the Greens? When the Soviet Union collapsed Teodor was depressed. He locked himself in his upstairs office, cried and talked endlessly into his dictation machine. John was saddened but not surprised.

He had seen how Marxists had usurped Marxism. He was repulsed by the comrades who fastened onto emancipatory discourse to build their own power base, ridicule the dreamers, and expel any dissenting voices. John never rejected Marx's vision, but he had seen how the political institutions had sucked out all the oxygen of hope.

Reflecting on a similar period of disillusionment in his life, Yanis Varoufakis recalled a friend who 'was a Marxist who despised most Marxists for using Marx's revolutionary rhetoric to abuse others, gain positions of influence, bed impressionable students, eventually take control of the politburo and throw anyone who questioned them into the gulag'.

John's house was a station in this ruined landscape. It was a place where conviviality not ideological correctness mattered. After the end of the Cold War, the sources of hope were damaged, and insecurity spread as capitalism colonised every detail of life. The pretence of upholding democratic values was shredded. The possibility that collective wellbeing should take precedence over private interests was made laughable. Margaret Thatcher's slogan 'there is no such thing as society' and the neoliberal mantra 'there is no alternative' became the new norms in mainstream public debates. We recognised that contemporary capitalism had colonised every aspect of commercial, civic and even private life. There was no longer the promise of escape to the art world. There were no spaces of exemption, only some occasions when capital had forgotten to plunge its knife. People had become exiled from their dreams of security without witnessing the drama of exit. It all happened slowly, with our drip-feed conformity, with our new politicians whose big goal was to pass the pub test, and then it also happened very fast, when new digital technologies demanded our endless consent.

10. Pig-shit Eurocentrism

A Greek-Australian art historian complained about the cost of Covid on the diaspora. Melbourne endured one of the longest lockdowns in the world. Australia had closed its borders. Even its own citizens were blocked from entering or leaving the country.

'Our lives are there as much as they are here!'

I felt for her. But then she said something that made me wince.

'I am Eurocentric!'

I understand her wish to hold onto the threads that tie her back to the homeland even if it emitted her parents. My friend is sophisticated. She relishes the folky dictions and is keen to preserve her mother's cuisine. Her peasant-based vocabulary and taste is also the foundation upon which a Protestant work ethic has developed. We are cursed over-achievers, and both of us feel confused when our friends in Greece don't see that it is rude to be three hours late for Sunday lunch.

But I do not think of myself as Eurocentric. I would rather vomit than adopt this term. It is not just a truncation of my connections to other parts of the world, but it also carries a revolting legacy of division and fake self-importance. The enlightened elites of Europe never thought that a peasant was a worthy participant in the public sphere. They hated the filth of the village. They had no time for callused and hunched men, whom they dismissed as deluded and indolent. And, in their eyes, the women were just carriers of scrofulous babies.

Kant was both a genius and well mannered. However, he too never imagined the need to have a dialogue with a peasant, and he regarded the natives of the colonies as unfortunate victims who had been trapped in the realm of redundant superstitions. Marx was not much better! Neither could imagine a time of reckoning with migrants in either the salons of Berlin or the mechanics institutes of Manchester.

Yet we were all peasants once.

I visited John in Paris on four occasions. He lived there for part of the year with Nella Bielski – a vivacious Russian author. She had high hopes for John. There was always an empty spot on her bookshelf – a reservation for his next novel, which, she also had no doubt, would finally convince the jury to award him the Nobel. John's book on longing and love *And Our Faces, My Heart, Brief as Photos*, was written in the times of the approach to and departure from Nella. It was inspired by the theme of time but got started by a gift from her – a notebook composed of sheets of thick brown paper that were similar to wrapping paper. The book is short. It has the tension and depth of an aphorism. However, it has the longing and tenderness of a melancholic love song. John said that sometimes it is the photo and not the train that brings the beloved to their rendezvous at the station. Their home was in Antony, a suburb near Orly airport.

In Antony John witnessed the bristling expansion of a multicultural metropolis. John was in every sense a cosmopolitan. Most at home when he was one among a multitude of strangers. Yet the hustle of everyday multicultural exchanges only came to him late in life. At the local pool he would find relief – floating in the water the grinding arthritic aches lifted. While dogpaddling he also enjoyed the conspiratorial glance of pensioners from every continent. He was finally getting closer to the people, who in his novel *Lilac and Flag*, he imagined from a distance. John had witnessed the journey of migrants. In *A Seventh Man* he followed their journeys from the villages in the south of Europe to the factories in the north. In the first two volumes of short stories in *Pig Earth* he reflected on the transformation of village life. In *Lilac and Flag* he imagined a mythic city of migrants called Troy. Here, amidst the cranes and crowds of Alexanderplatz, the children of migrants both search for love and survive by selling their blood.

The first time I visited John in Paris I rode there on my BMW

Boxer. When I travelled the breadth of France, from Calais to Quincy, I recorded the names of the successive villages on a single yellow sticky paper that was attached to my fuel tank. I could glance down at my simple map and never feel lost. The journey from the outskirts of Paris to his home involved so many turns that I need three stickers. When I arrived, the garden was in full summer bloom. I told John many diaspora stories. He roared with laughter when I began by confessing that I was once a stripper for the rich ladies of Toorak. On the corner of Toorak and Burke Roads was the premium antique shop. I was the stripper of the furniture that arrived in containers from England. After I disassembled and cleaned the tables and chairs, a carpenter called Len would tighten any defective joints. Then the French polishers, working with a potion made from the crushed wings of the Sri Lankan shellac beetle, would slowly and repeatedly apply layers of varnish until the surface was as viscous as a mirror. Len had a goatee beard and mullet haircut. He looked like a surfer with a paunch belly. During our breaks he studied the horse racing form guide in *The Truth*. The only time he spoke was when he told me, each and every day, that he wanted a meat pie with sauce for lunch.

A few weeks after I started work another man arrived. Fernando was from Portugal. He had a moustache like Manuel in *Fawlty Towers*, but unlike Manuel, he did not speak a single word of English. However, he had the most impressive bag of tools and photos to prove that he was a master carver of inlaid wooden designs. I looked at his innocent face and the scowling look of Len. I wondered how these two would now be forced to share a shed. The next day Fernando brought his lunch from home. Len ordered his usual. When I returned, I found Len and Fernando crouched underneath a large mahogany table. Silently and lovingly they both passed the right tool to each other.

I had been seeing John on and off for nearly twenty years. The last time I visited him with Nella in Anthony, my daughter Maya was with us. He prepared a feast, laughed raucously, spoke about an essay on Charlie Chaplin that he was working on, and then he took Maya into the study so that they could draw together. When John draws, he stares intensely, squinting into details, his body hunched over the pad, arms wide, sighing as he strokes the paper. The rubber is as active as the pencil, and if he is using charcoal all his fingers are smudged. His energy is relaxed but hyper-alert. Sizing up the subject like a front-row hooker entering the scrum. His drawings were both rugged and tender. They were the visual equivalent of Tom Waits's voice. Some of the charcoal lines were thick, and there were clouds of smudging in which lyrical quotations were inserted with a fine pencil. Maya was still a kid. Her hands moved on the notebook without evaluation. He loved this freedom. I hope, somewhere in her body, that this memory is there.

When Maya returned to school at the beginning of 2017, the principal announced a list of people who had passed away during the summer break. John Berger was one of the names of the people whose presence will, as the principal claimed, 'continue to shape the school'. Maya felt herself getting closer to the school and recalled the warm breath of a drawing lesson in the suburbs of Paris.

Australia was not just the Antipodes; it was for John almost beyond comprehension. John was a European. America was his opposite. He saw no contradiction between art and politics. He was not naïve enough to believe that the Soviet Union was Communist. However, he could not understand the violent breakup of Yugoslavia. As we stood at the barn door waiting for Louis and his load of hay, he pointed to the other side of the mountains.

'It is just there. I visited a few times, and it seemed to work quite peacefully.'

As for Africa, Asia, Latin America and Australia – his bike could never make it that far.

When I told my friend Lois McNay that I had sold my apartment in Manchester, quit my job and was heading back to Australia, temporarily, the line went dead.

'I guess I better come up and see you.'

'I don't have cancer!' I replied and laughed.

And yet the Antipodes had come early to John. At St Edward's boarding school, not far from Lois's college in Oxford, a teacher from New Zealand introduced John to the world of ideas. He was John's guide across the sensual frontier of eros and gnosis. John described their intimacy with discretion. The teacher met his parents. I later wondered whether John thought there might be some connection with his teacher from New Zealand and my background in Australia. But to him, this Antipodean teacher was more like the return of the prodigal. A rebel from the periphery who reaffirmed the values of the centre. By contrast, in John's eyes I was the son of Greek peasants. He could not reach out and connect the migrant story with the jagged layers of colonial dispossession. When I tried to put these stories side by side it left him speechless.

Just as we were about to enjoy an evening meal in Paris a Polish neighbour arrived. He looked at me and the other young man at the table.

'Who are these guys?'

John was at the head of the table, but his head dropped with a shy bow. Nella was standing and chirped up.

'These BEAUTIFUL BOYZ have both written books on JOOHHHN.'

Geoff Dyer, even when he is sitting, looks tall, angular and lazy. In his sloping way he leant across the table, curled his left eyebrow, and gave a wry droll Roger Moore smile. I looked bright-eyed and nervous, more like Harpo in the Marx brothers. John squished up his lips and squealed with embarrassment, but then with his two index fingers and thumbs tugged at the bottom of his shirt pockets – just over the spot where his nipples would lie. He let out a little chuckle and raised his forehead as if to toast himself.

I don't recall ever gossiping with John. There was small talk. Lists of chores and items to fetch from the market. But spending time dissecting another person's flaws was considered stupid and a waste of time. Unless, of course, any attempt at character assassination also carried with it the outline of a new trend, like Margaret Thatcher and the emergence of Thatcherism. If someone spotted such a figure in the landscape, then John was all ears. He would look for clues for the impact of politics on the way clothes were worn, or twitches expressed on the face, and gestures made by the hands. This was not gossip but the uncovering of the historical clues. He believed that ideas and ideologies were manifest on the body long before they became articulated as concepts. And so, for the discovery of such signs John would listen to the notes in the conversation like a piano tuner.

My father also despised gossip. He refused to trade in put downs, but he was the world's worst listener. If you were ever locked in debate with him, he could not help but interrupt. 'You finished.' You pointed out that this was rude and that you were *not* finished. 'Sorry, finish then, finish, and then I will tell you!'

11. How Many Fathers Before You Become Your Own Man?

John turned eighteen in the final year of World War Two. The boys from his school were expected to become officers. John had already run away to London and enrolled at art school. In defiance of his class privilege John served as a lance corporal with working-class lads and was briefly stationed at a training depot in Ballykelly, Northern Ireland.

A year after he died, I was in London, staying at the Goodenough Club in Mecklenburgh Square and reading *Here Is Where We Meet* (2005). In the essay 'Islington' he described the bombing during the Second World War. During the London Blitz he spent many nights with his fellow student Colette. They were staying in her flat in Guildford Place. Six decades later John recalled the view of Coram's Fields from her window in his essay.

I found myself on the same corner. In between us is the Foundling and Coram's Fields with its strict entrance sign: 'Adults are only allowed entry if they are accompanied by children.'

John and Colette drew all day, and at night, under the cover of blankets, they gave names to their anatomy – London for his recidivist erection and Damascus for her toes which he loved to tickle. The blitz continued.

I stood at the intersection of Guildford Street and Guildford Place, the only spot from which you could see Coram's Fields. Number 1 and 2 of the rows of terraced houses were gone. A bomb must have landed.

John was impressed that Louise Neri had flown from New York to Barcelona to introduce him to Juan Muñoz. Louise was Juan's dealer at the Gagosian Gallery in New York. She had carved out a specialist niche in producing books on a select group of artists. She had convinced Larry Gagosian that if her books helped persuade one client to buy an extra work, then that in itself would more than cover the book production costs. Juan had arrived from Madrid by train and John on his Honda. Louise and Juan were desperate for John to contribute to the book accompanying his next show. John was in Barcelona to launch the novel *To the Wedding*. Barcelona was the hometown of his daughter-in-law who died from AIDS. The previous night he read a passage in which the blind narrator Nikos Tsobanakos described the *zembekiko* dance.

John called Louise the 'shepherdess'. For him this was the ultimate 'Berger/Tsobanakos' compliment. Louise did not hear it that way.

When John and Juan met it was an instant love affair.

Juan shared the name of the protagonists in John's novels, Janos, Giovanni, Jean. In Barcelona wild mushrooms were in season. They had a feast and Juan gave John a flick knife.

My father's name was also Yianni/John. My father did not produce any writing. He barely completed the primary years of education. As a child he worked as a shepherd. When I was young, I looked away from my father. I recoiled from his repeated self-deprecating remarks: 'Don't be like me sonny, study, get a new life!' It was hard to overthrow a macho who both steps aside and sacrifices himself entirely for you. My father did not know what was ahead of me. He only hoped that by gaining a profession I would climb out of the mud and shit from which he came. This also meant that I did not know what a paternal figure looked like. My father was missing for most of the days. I did not notice the extent to which he supported and nourished the family. He returned from work late in the night. My mother was the force and compass of the house. I thought that I resembled her. As I grew older, I saw more and more of his face in my mirror. His eyes, and in particular his mother's eyes, were staring back at me. In my youth my face was more androgynous. By middle age I could see the likeness with my father grow in my jowls and in the broadening of my forehead. One morning, while shaving, I felt as if I had switched sides of the family. It was reassuring. I felt an ocean of tenderness lapping between us.

He was three years younger than John and during the war his job was to hide the neighbour's flock from the occupying Nazi forces. Only once did my father and I meet in his village. It was during the *panegyri* – the summer festival. Late one afternoon we walked out into the fields to find his favourite spring. The mountains had reforested since the peasant numbers had dwindled. Wolves and bears had returned. We each took a solid walking stick. While picking mushrooms two large shepherd dogs came bounding towards us. My father turned and said: put down your stick and be calm. The dogs circled us, remained vigilant, but they did not attack us. When the shepherd arrived, the dogs sat at our feet. The shepherd and my father recognised each other from their days in primary school. He looked at the large mushroom in my father's hand. Pulled the knife from his waist band and sliced in half. It bled blue.

'There is enough poison there to wipe out the whole village,' he said.

As Odysseus approached the hut of his old shepherd Eumaeus the dogs also barked with ferocity. Homer tells us that Odysseus also sat calmly and released the hold of his staff.

After my first semester of teaching at Manchester University in 1992 I collapsed with a serious flu. It took a week to recover. As I got back on my feet, I convinced my friend George Michelakakis to accompany me to Mount Athos. George was an artist, writer and activist. He was an inspiration when I began my research on migration and art in 1984. I helped him edit a journal in Melbourne on art and politics called *Chronico*. George had been living in Australia for twenty years when a neighbour had rung to tell him that his mother was on her death bed in hospital. He had left on bad terms. He wanted to be an artist.

She thought that this was the devil's work. She recruited a woman to remove the curse of an evil eye.

After the phone call George decided to return to Greece to farewell his mother. On arrival he barely recognised his neighbourhood in Piraeus. The small cottage was still standing. It was surrounded by apartments. The verdant hills were now all concrete. He opened the door. The stench of cat's urine and scattered piles of old newspapers was overwhelming. He left his bag and went to the hospital. His mother was in a ward with five other elderly women. He could not recognise her. He screamed her name.

She replied: 'My son, you have come home.'

The journey to the monasteries in Mount Athos was complicated. A train from Athens to Thessaloniki. In Thessaloniki there is an office where we arrange for a 'passport'. Then a bus to the border town of Ouranoupolis. Mount Athos is the third leg of a series of peninsulas that juts out from the region of Chalkidiki. At Ouranoupolis there is a ferry that will take us to the administrative capital Karyes. As the boat departed a dolphin skimmed the emerald sea. Then another joined to play in the game of chasing the wake. Their bodies moved with speed and grace, as if their conical form was one muscle. Approaching the jetty, we noticed that a row of monks stood out – silent and thin like cypress trees. They could see the boat getting closer, but their eyes made no indication that they saw any of us. Already I felt closer to the mammalian dolphin than the spirit of the monk. We had our papers checked and stamped. We could proceed to our first destination.

The path up the cliff top to Simonopetra monastery was steep and long. A soldier on leave was striding up ahead of us in a mad hurry. My companion, George, was suddenly transported to another world. The flowers and herbs on the verges were the same as those his mother harvested when the hills outside of Piraeus were teeming with flora. We were mercifully slowed down by his latent 'pharmacognosy'.

He stopped and recited the function of each herb that he had learned from his mother, who carried a medicinal tradition that includes Dioscorides's *De materia medica* from the first century CE.

A monk opened the gate. I wouldn't say that he greeted us, because the look in the monk's eye was both dismissive and detached. He received us without any words. I saw a hint of his yellow teeth behind his beard. These monks are known as Hospitallers. The title is a legacy of the Crusades. The Hospitallers originally cared for the sick and poor pilgrims. However, they soon became the most formidable military order and went on to colonise Rhodes, and then as far away as the Caribbean Islands. The Greek monks consider the Crusaders to have been a greater evil than Nazism. My travelling companion and I sat silently in a waiting room with a majestic view out towards the sea.

We entered our names, address, occupation in the registry.

The monk returned with a tray lined with a doily carrying water, Turkish delight, Greek coffee and raki.

When we had regained our breath, the monk gestured to show us to our room. He glanced at the registry. Noticing that I was a scholar, and my friend was an artist, he invited us for a conversation in the library.

This is the exact order of the rituals of hospitality that Homer described when Odysseus arrived in the gracious court of King Alcinous. Silence, cleansing, nourishment and identification.

In the library the monk opened a box and showed us his favourite icon.

'This is direct from God. It was not made by the hand of a man.'

'Why did God use the perspective of the Italian Enlightenment, and also include these miniatures in the background that look like they have a Turkish influence?' I asked.

The box was suddenly closed shut. We were pointed in the direction of the refectory and then he led us to our cells. The church was obvious. We were expected to be at all the services. Dinner was as sparse as the solitary icon in our room. The vegetables were fresh and the bread with dips was delicious, but a rector read passages from the Bible to remind us of the sin of gluttony. Above the entrance to our cells was a hand-painted sign:

'If you die before you die, then you will not die when you die.'

After ten days at Mount Athos, we returned to Thessaloniki. George and I were walking back to our hotel after a late dinner. Ten days in the company of monks and on a peninsula dedicated to the Virgin Mary and I was as horny as hell. Across the road two transvestites were leaving a bar and entering a waiting taxi. Their perfume wafted across the two lanes of traffic. I wanted to lean over and lower my head on a naked shoulder. I was spinning.

Towards the end of my father's life, I learned to recognise that his phrases were replete with litotes. The succinct and self-effacing phrases that structured my father's thoughts carried within them a rich seam of ideas. While the Enlightenment never came to their villages, it could be seen as a blessing. The brilliant ethnographer John Cuthbert Lawson claimed that they heard whispers of the theories of the ancient cosmos in the proverbs and love songs of the peasants. George Seferis, the Nobel Prize-winning poet, was unique in his ability to create poetry that combined the peasant's understatement and modernist structure.

I kissed red lips and my own lips were dyed red.
I wiped them with my handkerchief and it was dyed red.
I washed it in the river and the river was dyed red.
The shores were dyed red and the great sea.
An eagle flew down to drink the water and his feathers were dyed red.
Dyed red was half the sun and the full moon...

My father would stand in the garden and talk to the ground. Pointing and remembering, plotting out sections and planting seedlings – there was a logic to his order, rotation, pruning and supporting trestles. Placing the seeds was an artform and a dialogue with the earth. But unless I stood there, and did as he did, there was no chance to learn. It was never verbalised, let alone recorded. It was all in the rhythm of the land and the hands.

The same kind of resonances between antiquity, Christianity and humanism can be found in Montaigne's writing. Montaigne wrote in an era before rationality demanded hard formula and eternal truth. Like my parents he was somewhere between a dogmatic puritan and a Diogenes-styled libertarian. He wrote with candour and wry humour.

Greek peasant culture with its pounded-earth floors and mudbrick walls was deemed by the elites in Athens to be stuck in the past. Greece was a belated member of the modern world, and for this the elites were forever deflecting their own self-hate by projecting contempt on their 'retarded cousins' in the countryside.

I feel nothing but warmth towards my pagan ancestors but shudder at the coldness of my more recent Byzantine forebears. The pagans feel so close that I can almost touch them. Those Orthodox aliens creep me out. I find empty churches full of repose. After all, the church is modelled on the mother's womb. When I am alone, I have no problem following the cycle of the frescoes from the suffering martyrs on the perimeter to the pride of place for the Madonna behind the altar and the ascendent Christ in the dome.

Ways of Seeing seems new to each successive generation of students. At the beginning of the first episode in the TV series, John questions the relationship between the meaning of painting and the condition of vision. The screen is filled with close-ups of crowded scenes in a Greek Orthodox church. The Byzantines were challenged by the power of the *eikona* – the image. Icons first appeared as a continuation of the Roman pagan rituals of appeasement and thanksgiving. For instance, there is the story of how Lycomedes and Cleopatra had fallen victims to the evil eye. While Saint John was passing through Ephesus, he supposedly raised them from the dead. In gratitude Lycomedes commissioned a painting of Saint John and added candles, garlands and incense. On a return visit to Lycomedes's house Saint John noted the persistence of the pagan Roman style of veneration. However, rather than ordering the destruction of the painting he summoned a mirror to confirm its likeness. Liking what he saw, he declared that Jesus was the true painter who could use colour to reveal the soul's virtues. For almost a century the Byzantines banished and burned all icons – they were the original iconoclasts. Then came the most significant philosophical rationalisation of the whole of the Byzantine civilisation. A hierarchical distinction was made between veneration and worshipping. Icons could be venerated if the faithful recognised that only God could be worshiped.

The Byzantines settled the question of how icons could be approached in a church. This served them well for over a millennium. Church was practically the only place where most people encountered an image. It was not until the beginning of the twentieth century when the art historians like Aby Warburg pondered the presence of an image and then a generation later social and media theorists like Walter Benjamin and Marshall McLuhan revisited the question on the consequence of images. Benjamin revived the idea of aura and McLuhan showed that the communication was not confined to nodes in the terrestrial networks of the global village but led all the way to the celestial cosmos.

Today images saturate our everyday environment. In a secular world we rarely speak of worshiping and venerating images, we like and love, appreciate and admire, we are inspired and repulsed, we follow or delete, we link and post, we mash and forward. The role of the image has exploded. Our dexterity has been extended. However, is our visual literacy as subtle on a conceptual scale as it is adept in its technical reach? When I reflect on the diaspora of images that rip open Greek identity, I wonder: 'Who is this Greek? Why am I not offended by the transgression of my ethnos?' I feel the waves lapping and receding. I am vulnerable and indifferent to absence. I don't see myself in the pages of the classics and yet I feel pride that others think my ancestors are there. I am neither marble nor papyrus. I think it is normal to be confused and disconnected.

John's and Tim Neat's film *Play Me Something* was set on a bleak watery landscape at the terminal of the Hebridean island of Barra. In this film an assortment of people is waiting for a plane to Glasgow. Tilda Swinton is luminous and the gruff poet Hamish Henderson is a perfect counterpoint. John appears dressed in a white shirt, dark tie, suit and hat. He enthrals them with a story of a Venetian love affair.

I was married to Victoria Lynn in Venice – the 'Queen of Cities'. After our wedding party came out of the Café Imagina I longed to reach out and touch you. In the morning, we had the official ceremony in a civic building by the Rialto. We had taken a tour of *la bella citta,* our friends and family stopping at preselected spots to make their own declarations to love. After lunch I danced the *zembekiko* – twirling through the vortex of trinkling bouzouki sounds. In the evening a boat had been scheduled to pick us up for a tour of the lagoon. I wanted John, Yves and Beverly to be there with Teodor, Pavel, Hetti, Sean, Diego, my brother Vasilli, mother Eleni and father Yianni, and Victoria's mother Lily.

Heading out of the Café Imagina and walking towards Campo Santa Margherita we approached three minstrel Romanian gypsies. One was in the middle with his accordion. My mother and father recognised the tune – 'The White Dove' from the film *The Boy and the Dolphin* starring Sophia Loren and Alan Ladd. The 1950s Italian musical films were big hits and the songs had been dubbed in Greek. In a reflex my mother and father burst into song and dance on the *calle.* My father dropped all the euros in his pockets.

The cinema had come to the villages after the war. White sheets would be set up in front of the *plateia* and in the summer nights the young and old would gather. In the neighbouring towns of Argos and Kastoria new theatres were christened with edifying names – Rex, Apollo, Olympion, Cosmo and Odeon. For five drachmas you could see Gina Lollobrigida. By the next day all the girls knew the songs. My mother would walk past the *kafenion*, the only place with an LP turntable, and hover in a demure way. In one hearing she would get it. While planting and harvesting, the fields were full of song. And at night, her Uncle Simeon would hold all the children captive with his stories of ogres and princesses. In the winter Simeon would get up early, carve a path in the snow, and the kids from both houses would each tuck a piece of wood under their arm, and make their way to school. As they arrived, they placed their little log by the school's furnace.

After the generation of my parents the villages went quiet. The fields by the Aliákmon River were now ploughed by German tractors. When the border with Albania opened migrants came in, to fill some small part of the hole left by others. I saw Albanian men staring into the *kafenion* while Greek men played cards inside. European Union agricultural subsidies had made the sons of peasants rich. One young arsehole waved his temporary winnings like a bunting in the wind. The widows still had memories of their migration from the Pontus. They pulled the trunks from under their beds and handed out coats and boots. My grandmother did not like seeing me walk around in Doc Martens shoes. She lured me into town to buy me the fashionable cowboy boots. I didn't want to dress like those jerks with black curly mullets. In the fields small campfires burnt in the night. People started locking their houses.

At around a quarter past the hour the bus came through my grandmother's village. The bus stop was next to the *kafenion*. In the daytime the older men held court in this little parliament. Broad-shouldered and wrinkled, they stared into space and listened to each other. Their suit jackets sitting on their backs, shirts buttoned tight, and chins resting on the handle of their walking sticks. When the bus arrived, I deferred stepping up so that an older woman could board. She ran next door to summon her husband. The driver was new. He departed instantly. As I took my seat, I saw an old man emerging from the *kafenion*. He then stood still, and the woman chased the bus down the dirt road. She was not the passenger but she cursed the novice driver.

The week before our wedding I had been sending pleading emails. Finally, the day before the event, the answer had come that John was not well enough to make the overnight train trip. Beverly even chided me for being pushy.

John sent three little doggerels to the lagoon with love.

To make a hole
through
a stone
to thread it
wear it
bespeaks immortality
the stone may be
language
the hole poety

Epithalamium for Nikos and Victoria
Do dolphins leap?
Definitely but they need the sea
Below two of them.
Then drinking their ecume
they do
their closed eyes
open as horizons

red poppies already here
beloved body already sore
to our foreheads apply
the cool salt of Wieliczka

I sat by the Lions from Delos that guard the gates to the Arsenale and felt that something was incomplete. The words were beautiful, uplifting and tender, but I was sulking. I was craving your laughter and missing your arm around my shoulder. Victoria had already prepared herself and tried to offer me the balm of perspective.

'He can't be everywhere. Look up and look where you are.'

The sun and sky dappled in the reflection of water and stone. I hate being a tourist. I enjoy other cities when I have an interesting job to do there. A holiday is when work is going well. A sunset is more satisfying when your body feels the worth of the day's strain. In the village with John the labour of haymaking was a form of recharging. Venice is different. It was made for the pleasure in transactions. It is a mecca for art, but regardless of what is in the galleries, it is the city itself that glistens like the lustre of an ancient mosaic. There is also a reassuring pleasure in finding, year after year, the same vendors, with slightly more grey hair, selling shiny *melanzane* from the barge with green shade, just as it is comforting to know that Rocco is still scooping chips onto the same plastic plates to accompany the Aperol spritz that you have just ordered.

Our bedroom was in the loft. Heavily stained wooden beams supported the terracotta roof. The house was built at a time when Venice was a global trading empire. The citizens of Serenissima had outposts across the Byzantium and their sailors plundered the forests along the Dalmatian coastline. Lying in bed, my dreams and residual thoughts were punctuated by the knots and cavities in the wood.

I awoke from a dream.

I love you.

I miss you.

I need you.

Moments before my friends all came closer, collectively put their hands on my shoulder.

Victoria was startled: 'Why are you screaming?'

Still in my nocturnal delirium I told her, 'I am shouting because it is market day today, as it is every Tuesday and every other Thursday.'

She said: 'There are no local markets in Venice.'

I fall back into a deep dream. John is speaking to me.

Come to my house, stay, the view to the sea is endless.

Sitting on his verandah was like dwelling in the delicious limbo between dream and reality.

The railings are firmly grounded. The shade is gentle. The cushioned seat that backs up against the wall is enticing.

Come to be with me.

I am there – the ground is beneath our feet, and beyond, hangs the horizon of twin sea-sky blues.

In the dream I see myself wondering. It feels strange but I also see myself continuing to dream: *How long can this last? When have I overstayed?*

Just before Christmas lunch in 1994 John's daughter Katya turned to me and looked deeply into my eyes.

'You are becoming one of the family.'

She was there at Geneva airport when John first picked me up. She had welcomed me into her life with Orestis in Athens. But at this time of the year there was no hay to be made. I was not there to do an interview. My book had been published. She was probably wondering: who will sleep in the back room? How many gifts should she have brought?

I thought to myself: why did I need to keep coming back to John's village? Was this return a reboot of a connection to my own ancestral place? The house in Quincy was not an idyll. It was a spur to find a place of repose. I did not feel a calling to be back in the Greek mountains. However, a new start, near the Aegean was swelling inside me. Houses are extensions of our bodies. Our dreams stay there. Blood seeps into the floors and walls without a trace. The mirrors hold everything. If I found such a home, maybe my child would one day feel that this is where her story begins.

Is it the view, or the lingering smell of labour that makes a house feel like home? I dreamed of being at one with the master, but so does he. The other in us and the eye that looks from beyond the master's house summons another leaving.

During that harvest in 1995 the rain would not stop. Beverly instructed us to paint the kitchen interior and wooden shutters. Beverly chose from a traditional colour scheme. John was already dreaming of another house in Sardinia, where Gramsci was born. A land he described as belonging to 'stone and shepherds', that conveyed an age even older than 'Greek and Egyptian geometry'. My mind went to an undefined place in Greece – somewhere I could build my own house, away from my father's mountain village, start a new line. John could see a house that far away, but not one further than the Aegean.

The spring after the wedding Yves sent a long letter full of details of his new life as a father. He expressed sincere regret that they had missed coming to Venice, and as a gift, he included a portrait of me on canvas.

'Even if I see many "problems" in the way it is painted, I can't re-work it. It tells something about a moment: when a young boy starts to paint the portrait of a friend. A friend to which he can say everything... during long walks at night. It stayed a long time in my parent's kitchen before I finally wrote this letter and decided to send it. I think we all enjoyed living with it. Maybe we saw it as a piece of what we all have inside: affection for you, love. That won't go away with the painting, and maybe it can carry some to your house.'

John's house was not a destination. It was not a house for disciples and apostles. He wanted his interlocutors and friends to be close and he would always smuggle gifts into your bags as you were leaving. One year, I tried to resist the insertion of a bottle *Châteauneuf du pape* – my prize from the pigeon-toss game. It was pointless, trying to refuse the innocence of his joy. In his blue shirt and silver hair, he waved farewell like a Greek flag.

A migrant's eye, yes, that now seems obvious, but what is it? Many scholars with a grander vision than mine have attempted to give a definition, or at least note some of its characteristic. Dante pointed out that when you leave home, everything seems to be odd, even the bread tastes different. Nietzsche hated stay-at-home types, and encouraged people to leave town, just to see how small the town's cathedral really was. Calvino had a good nose for the smells on foreign streets, some would make you gag, others would lead you into the forbidden shadows. Simmel noted that the stranger's mentality was forever oscillating, comparing the spaces of here and there, crosschecking between the time of now and then. What these great minds all saw was that displacement was essential for critical thinking. It was not just a matter of contrast and evaluation, but also a willingness to challenge the singular measures that each culture produces for its own making sense of things.

John preferred the unsettled and disoriented view to the smug perspective of the entitled. His eyes were flicker-fast, intense in their pursuit of dark depths and eager to span the spring horizons.

John chose to leave his native England. He expressed an affinity with the appreciation of ideas and culture in France, but he was not part of any Parisian club of scholars, artists and writers. He lived between the village and the suburb. No one has ever called him a migrant or a refugee. Was he an exile? There is such a moral burden that comes with these labels, and I am not sure he bothered to check. His energy was in contesting the hierarchies that asphyxiate us all.

John trusted the migrant's eye. Of course, some migrants move in search of fame and fortune. Most, however, leave because they have no choice. They leave to survive, to find a glimmer of freedom.

I was driving in Athens with my father. We pulled off the ring road and stopped at the intersection of the entrance to the suburb of Peristeri. Sheltered from the midday sun were small groups of men, some selling little plastic handheld fans. The underpass was littered with pigeon shit, small mounds of old shoes and bundles of fake designer bags.

'Why would you leave home in the prime of your life to come to this!'

My father replied: 'Imagine how much worse life can be elsewhere for you to want to stay here.'

I recalled the moment I said: 'Dad, we are eating your favourite meal tonight.'

He replied: 'All food is equal.'

'Why don't you have a favourite?'

'Not when there are others who have none.'

When we passed beggars and street peddlers, he emptied his pockets. I was more conflicted. Nietzsche confessed that he didn't like giving to beggars, but he also was not proud to walk by and do nothing.

John looked into the eyes of migrants not only to convey his empathy for their suffering, but it was also an inquiry – he tried to read the signs of the journey that they had undertaken. He often changed the circumstances in his life to have a closer look at how life had changed for others. He joined the circle of exiles and emigres in London. He followed the journey of migrants from the rural south to the industrial north of Europe. He lived with the peasants in the alps of France. He needed to grasp the truth of their point of view, and in this, he was sure that there was also a measure of what really counts.

John, can you still hear me, are you near, the story is close to its end.

I received the message of your death while I was on a family holiday at Stradbroke Island. We were staying at a house without internet connection. Every morning, I would go out and get fresh bread. Just as you did in Mieussy. Pulling up at a car park in Cylinder Beach the signal returned to my phone. Tick, tick, emails, and messages rolled in. I checked my phone and found the news from Yves. There were also several other messages from friends around the world. It was morning. The air was still moist. The windows to my car were still closed. I was in shock. Suddenly, there wasn't even an inch of air left in my car. I had to jump out. I could not move. What to do?

It was not long since we had last seen each other in Paris. We spoke on the phone the day after we had dinner together. You said you wanted to send me an essay on Chaplin. I was enthusiastic. You added: 'No need to send back any feedback.' It felt strange and cutting. We ended the call by talking about Bastille Day.

Yes, you were old John, but in the twenty years I knew you, you never seemed frail or exhausted.

My breath in the car park at Cylinder Beach started to settle and I began thinking. I rang Yves and he told me about the details for your funeral. I then rang my travel agent who found a flight from Brisbane to Geneva that would get me there in time. I could buy winter clothes from the airport, hire a car, and get to the house before the procession began. I was about to accept the booking when I realised that my passport was in Melbourne. Retrieving it would add another day of travel.

Yves sent beautiful photos of the procession from Quincy to Mieussy. People came from all the points of Europe. The whole village paused, and the town joined the procession. At the reception Katya and Yves had made a circle of books that had been published in his lifetime. And they offered a hearty soup to feed the cold mourners. The photos had a propulsive force. The crisp air from the mountain overtook me and for a moment it overpowered the humid heat of Stradbroke Island.

A few months later Yves sent a parcel of books. It included *Confabulations*. The first essay is entitled 'Self Portrait' and it recounts your lifelong wrestling match with metaphors. Your books have been my companions for almost all of my adult life. There has always been one next to me, and your words speak from the horizon that my hopes aim for. My first reflection on the experience of reading *Permanent Red* and *Ways of Seeing* was that I had found my guide. Here was my world and the other world I wanted to live in. A companion and trailblazer of a common quest. And now there will be no more new books by you...

In 1988 celebrations were conducted for the bicentenary of Australia's colonial history and national identity. The journalist and documentary filmmaker John Pilger was at the peak of his powers. He was commissioned to make a four-part series on the history of the nation.

As a cadet journalist Pilger's first job was to go to the port and return with any news from the incoming boats. What stayed in his mind were not the stories from the home country, but the arrival of young migrants from southern Europe. He titled his reflection on the history of Australia – *The Last Dream: Heroes Unsung* (1988).

At the time I was living in a shared household in Cambridge. By accident, I caught some scenes of the documentary as it was screened on ITV. For a split second I thought I saw an image of my mother. How could it be? I tried to put it out of my head. Months later as I was about to head back to Australia for a brief holiday, I wrote to my friend Scott McQuire asking if he could get a copy of the TV series on a video cassette. He dutifully delivered it to me soon after my arrival. I still had my doubts, so I left the video cassette near the TV cabinet at my parent's house.

One Saturday afternoon, after a little disagreement with my mother, I decided to play the cassette. She had just left the house and I thought it might help me calm down. Midway through the first episode there is a close-up of a porthole. As it opens the camera zooms in. The Blaupunkt TV screen was filled with an image of a young woman with a low-cut laced shirt and a dangling gold cross as she pokes her head out. There is a look of trepidation in her eyes.

It is my mother.

The previous shots included a wide sweep of the deck with young women all wearing white gloves and waving with joy. Followed by a close-up of the name of the ship – *Waterman*. This brief sequence is followed by an aerial view of the pier. Slowly the camera focuses on two men. One is a much thinner version of my Uncle Stergio and next to him is another man in a beautiful light-coloured suit carrying flowers.

I don't recognise this man.

When my mother returns, I sit her down in front of the TV and play the cassette. Somehow, she is not taken aback. Like a retired actress, she simply draws more heavily on her cigarette and declares – 'You see how beautiful I was!' Then wistfully pronounces the name *Waterman*. I rewind the cassette and freeze at the image of my uncle and the other man on the pier.

I ask: 'But who is this man?'

The better question would have been, how did the editor cut the scene with my mother and paste it next to my uncle on the pier.

My mother looked at the still shot of the young man, and after a long sigh she proceeded to tell me the story of her journey to Australia. In her village she had fallen in love with a gambling man who was a regular at the card games in the *kafenion*. It would have been tabooed to be in an open courtship with him, but somehow messages had gone back and forth, and an agreement was reached that they should meet in Australia. My mother had accepted a free passage on what was known as a bride ship. There were so many Greek bachelors in Australia that the government offered free trips to single women who would be interested in marriage. Her cousin Stergios had sponsored her, and his friend Kosta was willing to propose.

My mother accepted the invitation but made no commitment. She had other plans. Kosta was a very courteous and gracious man. Unfortunately, he died of a heart attack soon after. My mother was still dreaming of the arrival of her gambling conspirator. Stergio was furious at her rejection of Kosta and asked her to leave the house. She wore out two pairs of heels on the cobbled streets of Richmond looking for new lodgings and eventually found a job in a biscuit factory in Abbotsford.

When Stergios died my mother asked me to drive her to visit his surviving siblings. I saw a photo of my mother's uncle Simeon. The man who lovingly called her 'little shit'. Beside Simeon was a photo of her grandfather – the famed cushion-maker Lefteri.

On the way home she expressed gratitude towards her cousin Stergio for initiating her passage to Australia.

'We left our villages. We did not become *letchides* – dirty ones.'

She recalled a story in the village when a dog had fallen into a dry well. It was yelping and the men found a long rope. Stergio had immediately volunteered to go down the well.

'When I saw him trying to do this crazy thing I burst into tears. I ran over still bawling out my eyes and threatened to tell his father if he went down.'

Stergio was more scared of his father than he was desperate to show off in front of the other men.

In a tone of forgiveness, she added: 'Blood is thicker than water.'

Her gambling man never arrived. Eventually she met my father. She came to the sensible conclusion that he would be a good father for her children. In a more recent version of the story, she insisted that she rejected the gambling man in her village because he was pig-headed.

A few years later Ana Kokkinos made the film *Head On* (1998), based on Christos Tsiolkas's novel *Loaded* (1995). It included the same archival footage that John Pilger had used. On the full silver screen of an art-house cinema, there is that opening of a porthole, she is staring out into a new world. I saw the film more than once. On the second occasion I took my mother. Once again, she sighed, at her journey, her youth, and perhaps, the cosmos.

I wanted to be a writer. I wanted the names and stories that my mother and father recited to find a home in writing. These lives deserved the dignity of contemporary art and French philosophy. I passed through their lives and worked with George, Don, Tony, Teodor, Rasheed and Pavel. To find my own voice I needed to leave Europe.

In my dream of you in Venice there is a last hug. One that holds all time of the past and all future humanity.

Come inside.
Leave your coat and scarf by the fire.
Here. Take my seat. I will get another bowl.
Thank you for this bottle.
We will open it later.
Do you have any jokes from where you have come?
Yes. But the punchline only works if you had been there!
So. Let's laugh to missing out!
We are back in the village.

As the night deepens, the damp boots slowly dry, our shoulders rock and merge together, and a new line furrows across our foreheads. In the barn up the hill the cows close their liquid eyes. A heaviness is resting on straw. Louis turns off the news. The clock in John's kitchen ticks and the bottle is opened.

12. Return to Quincy

In 2023 I returned to John's village. John, Beverly, Louis and Andre had all passed away. Yves had purchased the house that Louis and Lina owned. Louis was thrilled that his 'son' would stay in the village. He used a large portion of the proceeds of the sale to gift Yves with the purchase of the slates to build a new roof. Yves and his partner Sandra spent two years renovating the house. The downstairs *cave* and stable were now integrated with the main house. A beautiful wall of books ran along the spine. Central heating was installed. The walls were waterproofed, and the smell of wide pine floorboards still wafted. A gallery space was introduced in the cathedral of the barn. The studio was untouched, but a printing room and storage space were meticulously added. Most of the skilled workers from the neighbouring villages were recruited. Many of the cupboards and much of the furniture were exactly where they were when I first visited. The house, which was built before the region was incorporated into the French Republic, stood bold and seemingly unchanged.

I was coming to Quincy in the middle of the summer. Most of the hay had already had its first cut. Yves was waiting for me at Geneva airport. He was wearing his special Nick Cave t-shirt in honour of the fact that I introduced him to this music. We hugged and kept saying, 'Good to see you, bastard!'

The day before, I was in Athens. My brother Vasilli had taken me to lunch at Dionysos restaurant. We sat just below the entrance to the Parthenon and barely fifty metres from where Saint Paul delivered his lecture on the evils of paganism. The Stoics and Epicureans had come to listen to this babbler. They rarely agreed on anything, but on this day, the philosophers from the rival schools looked to each other, and said:

'Yeah, yeah, we have heard this all before. It won't catch on.'

My brother and I were eating with the former defence minister, and with a wry sense of irony the former minister said:

'There are one hundred and forty-seven Greek pilots today working for Turkish Airlines. Can you imagine if the pilot on Aegean Airways said: "Good evening, ladies and gentlemen. This is your captain, Hakim Bey... " All the Greeks would run off the plane.'

Sometimes I reflect on how much the Greeks are in denial about racism. They think only empires produced racism to explain the way they imposed their ideology and justify their subjugation of other people. They think they are exempt from this criticism because they are a small and weak state. They play the victim, but they too collude in the same bully things to marginalise migrant workers and distance themselves from responsibility towards refugees.

The taxi driver who drove me to the airport was chatty. He asked where I was from, what I did for a living. I told him I did research on art and migration. He then started to tell me his life story.

He came from Albania as a kid, walking for seven days, through the same mountains my grandmother crossed.

He told me of how the border guards and solders tortured and traumatised kids for sheer sport and laughter. Tying them upside down on trees, then cutting the branch and laughing as they fell on their heads. How Greek famers exploited the labourers. Feeding them meat out of cans, which the men thought was 'conserves' but was in fact dog food. Then at the end of the season rather than paying them, they called the police and had them deported.

Is it any surprise that they came back looking for revenge and got themselves 'organised' by the mafia?

In 1993 I saw these things for myself in my mother's village. At first the widows were crying and sad to see a new generation of *kaumenoi* – the burnt ones, referring to the survivors from the Asia Minor disaster and, in particular, to the victims in the burning of Smyrna. Then rumours spread. Small fires got started by men who had fallen asleep in the fields. The young men of the village, who thought that their Ganni contrast-stitch cowboy boots and curly black mullets made them *manges* – dudes, set out to taunt and thrash the skinny ones.

Albanians are the engine of Greece, and I am constantly apologising to them. My flight was delayed so I texted Yves on WhatsApp.

We chatted in the car. The drive from the airport to the village was familiar. The street signs had changed. Restaurants had added new neon signs. Once again, the Tour de France had just passed through. Locals had festooned the verges with the name of their favourite rider. The number 74, referring to the department of Haute-Savoie, was proudly chalked on the bitumen.

After passing the quarry at Saint-Jeoire we turned into the small road that led to the villages of Anthony, Ley and Quincy. It was just four kilometres. I wound down my window. Instantly, the whole haymaking season came rushing up my nose. I was thrust back by the combination of the scent of cut grass and the re-growth – the *regain* – which is somewhere between toast and the smell of those wheat bags you warm in the microwave when you have a sore stomach. My head rolled in the front seat of the car. Then as we opened the door I felt as if I was in the barn. There is a farmhouse next door to Yves which has over a hundred cows sleeping and living in a luxurious stable. These young farmers have consolidated the cows for the whole village. Where there were ten small farmhouses, now there is one large complex. Soon the cows will be milked by robots. But the shit and piss do not go away.

As we arrived Sandra was sitting in the garden chatting and laughing with the neighbours. I could barely understand anything.

In the past I could join a few dots. Bits of conversation were switched into English. I was offered pâté made from the pig that Yves and his neighbours had reared. A glass of wine, a few slices of Tomme cheese, and the boys recalled the stories I had told them about AC/DC and Nick Cave.

When I first met Sandra, she was living with her grandmother and working in a supermarket. She was petite with strong arms as well as being smart and focused. Yves and Sandra have been together for twenty-five years. She now works as a teacher in a Steiner kindergarten near Geneva. When her grandmother died, she got a small inheritance, and decided to use the money to buy a cello.

When I wake up the next morning Sandra is sitting in the same garden seat playing her cello. I am upstairs in John's old bedroom. The room has been converted for their daughter Melina. John would write at a small table with a checquered cloth over it. He used a Sheaffer fountain pen and A4 paper. Yves had hoped that Melina would stay as long as possible. After high school she travelled and enrolled in medical school at the University of Geneva. Her room looks like she was there yesterday. She told Yves I can use it as long as I don't touch any of her hair products.

Yves has taken his son Vincent to the dentist. There is a lull. The sparrows are quietly twitching among the seedbeds.

I keep seeing the house as it was with Beverly and John, and admiring how it has become with Sandra and Yves. They have both improved it and kept the old one alive. So many little links. Clock, barometer, cupboards and posters, such as the poster of the painting by Jean-François Millet, *Des Glaneuses* (1857), depicting three peasant women gleaning a field of wheat. Vincent is like an acrobat. He does tumbles straight after lunch and dreams of being a motorcross rider. The house has new kid stuff, musical instruments, and paintings by Yves.

There was a heatwave when I left Athens but here it is raining. I had forgotten how quickly the weather changes in the Alps. There is a new sign announcing the village at the hairpin corner outside Yves's house: Quincy, alt 755 m, Montagnes du Giffre.

The stern mountains which look down on you can quickly pull up a veil of cloud and drop rain. It was always infuriating for Louis as he tried to anticipate the weather when cutting the hay.

These mountains are so solid, I still find them a bit intimidating. I feel surrounded in a way that makes me feel less than lonely. I see how small I am, but also feel that I am within them, not apart.

The memory of John and Beverly is everywhere in the house. The white bird, a little sculpture that peasants carved out of two pieces of wood. The maquettes of distended figures by his dear friend Juan Muñoz. The portraits of John by Yves and so many other artists that loved and admired him. John and Beverly paid little attention to creature comfort. They would love the house as it has become, but they were just as comfortable in the old one. They kept the domestic things very simple. For some visitors it was a bit too agricultural. My body adjusts very fast.

The strong scents I felt yesterday, I have to search for on my second day. Now I am noticing more the chittering and chirping of the swallows and sparrows. Today I can see how close the houses are to each other, the moisture of the soil, the abundance of green in the vegetation, the density of the forest, and the stony ridges and ice-capped mountain peaks.

John was convinced that the life of the peasant in the village was ending. His trilogy *Into Their Labours* was a testament to the cunning and resilience of the peasants, but it was also a eulogy. He was right. No one farms the old way anymore. When I came to visit shortly after his death in 2017, it felt like his predictions would come true for the whole of the village. Many more houses had been abandoned. The town of Mieussy was in decline. You could not even buy fresh bread and chocolate croissants anymore.

Bauge, the dandy butcher with fine silk cravats and thick tweed jackets, had closed his shop soon after I stopped visiting in the late 1990s. He even closed the café which he owned. He put both on the market. He was a proud man and knew his value. Some said his price was too high. The shops remained empty for two decades. He waited. Every year he opened the café for the requisite week so that he could retain the license. His shops were in a prime position: overlooking the valley and next to the neoclassical town hall. Months before the covid pandemic a young couple bought both shops and used the period of lockdown to convert them into an elegant bar and café. During this brief period the town experienced a rebirth. Tourism to the Alps increased. People found new ways to work from home. Some were prepared to commute to Geneva. A small group of anarchists survived a winter in an old farmhouse tucked away at the edge of the forest.

I wanted to treat Yves and Sandra to a celebratory meal. Sandra refused. 'You are our guest, Nikos!' Yves booked a table at the restaurant that was once Bauge's butcher shop. Bauge still lived upstairs and could probably hear us. We sat outside under a plane tree, in perfect summer weather. No mozzies. I had raw tuna for a starter, a steak cooked in butter, so juicy and creamy, followed by a slice of tarte with summer berries. Yves and I polished off a bottle of red. A recipe for much pleasure and much snoring after.

In the morning Sandra complained: 'I did not sleep so well. But I got up opened the kitchen door and there was a shooting star.'

Some reward for enduring the orchestra in the bedroom.

This morning the birds were less raucous. Just the odd bird chirping and tweeting. I also struggled to sleep.

The following evening Yves and I took our soul walk. The route is the same that we took when he was a kid. We head up the hill from Quincy to the old dairy at St Denis. Then turn right in Rue du Crot, passing through some pretty hamlets. We meander down into the village of Messy, with its beautiful wooden houses, massive stone bread ovens and vast stables. From there we zigzag through Ley, where the carpenters build chalets. This drops us onto the road back to Quincy. Having just left the Balkan world, which like Manchester and London, is not known for its pride in maintaining the streets, I am struck that not a single plastic bottle top, crushed beer can or food wrapper is to be found for the duration of the journey. There is not even a single pothole in the bitumen.

It is a two-hour walk, and we talk in the dark. We are open about our hearts, but this year, I told him that something had happened that I could not discuss. He kept prodding. I told him forcefully that I could not yield but that I wanted him to know that I had an earth-shaking experience. As I said this, a huge flock of black birds were disturbed at the top of a forty-foot pine tree. The squawking and flapping seemed like a desperately noisy struggle against nature and gravity. We then saw them bolting across an open field. There must have been at least twenty or more. Yves looked up and conceded: 'That is impressive. It must be big.'

I said: 'You see, if you ask any more questions, it could be lightning next.'

We laughed and we talked about Blondie, his first love. I was moved by his story of finding her on Instagram and their reacquaintance. They had met at a concert. She was on stage singing and looking at him. She was a bit older and guided him. Now she is a single mother and a full-time nurse. Yves invited her to a concert to meet Sandra and gave her the recent CD by PJ Harvey.

I asked about John's friend Andre.

'He died of heart attack. It was a shock to the village. But both his children, Chrystal and Giles have moved back.'

Yves read my mind.

'Yes, she is still very beautiful.'

Giles had fallen in a love with a woman who was married with three kids. Her husband knew that she was in love with Giles, but he could not accept that she would not come back to him. He was not nasty, just stubborn in his delusion. Giles's patience won. This theme in the walk was pressing hard on the topic I announced but could not reveal. Yves seemed particularly buoyant and at ease with himself. Almost all the houses in the village are now full. The life in the village has been reborn. The flinty character of the Savoyard peasants is still there. If a neighbour's washing machine breaks down, they know that another is available. There is a delicate balance between rugged discreetness and unquestioning hospitality. Car keys are left in letter boxes. Many of the houses have been renovated or subdivided. However, from the outside the practical shape and material texture have remained as it was.

In 2017 I had walked up the hill to Louis's house with Yves. We took the short cut. The house was unchanged, but its tempo felt as if it had come to an abrupt halt. There were tools left on the doorstep. The cows had been sold off. Louis was in hospital recovering from a heart attack. When he died in 2022 Yves contacted me by Zoom. As he spoke, I leaned across my desk and pull into view a framed photo from my shelf. It was Louis in his Christmas party hat, trying his best not to look glum. In my memory those five years between hospitalisation and death collapsed into a single point. I could not have imagined a new glorious arc in Louis's life.

On the third morning of my visit in 2023 Yves informed me that he had to do some chores with a neighbour. I said:

'I will walk to Louis's house.'

'Good idea! Go the long way around.'

It was a beautiful time of the day, and the temperature was around twenty-eight degrees Celsius. I walked backwards up the hill so I could enjoy the views of Mont Blanc – the tallest mountain in Europe. It was a surprisingly clear view, only the final pinnacle was smudged by a cloud, the other snow-capped peaks were clear. A rare sighting.

As I turned onto the road to the house the scene suddenly felt as if it had been underused. The fields have been purchased by the Bertrands. They are well maintained. But along the verges the bitumen was cracked. The grass in the cracks was longer than I remembered it. Poppy flowers sprouted here and there. Some wild lavender and daffodils. The trees were covered in lichen. The creek that bisects the field was trickling at reduced speed. Earlier I had seen buzzards and black birds circling in the thermals, looking for prey in the open fields. A cat had got ahead of them and was fiendishly prodding and tearing at a rodent in a hole. A young hawk was screeching to assert its dominance over the sky. Not quite big enough to scare anyone.

As I got to Louis's house I was greeted by the new owners. Louis owned two houses, and two garages on this block. The second house he rented to holiday makers. This house was now occupied. A man was starting up his tractor and two women were working on a vegetable patch, cucumbers, zucchini and tomatoes. I told them I was a friend of Louis and John. They smiled and wondered why I had come up the long way.

Louis's main house was a shock. The front entrance had been renovated. It looked like someone wanted to make it presentable and easy to clean. The door to the main entrance had been polished. The wooden palings on the balcony were painted red and yellow. The barn area, basin and garages were dilapidated. It looked like an incomplete holiday house. It was no longer a working farmhouse.

On our soul walk Yves told me that in his last few years Louis met a woman called Joelle. When they were young, they were classmates. He was always fond of her but, like all the women in the village of his generation, she moved to the city and married a factory worker. When she was widowed, they met again, and the old flame was rekindled. She lived on the other side of France, near the Atlantic coast. Apart from his military service Louis never left his village area. He travelled to her in a shared car but got sick on the journey. She nursed him. When he recovered, he had to get his ride back to the mountains. He was close, but he did not see the sea. She came to visit and stay with him. These were the happiest and most tender years of his life. On his eightieth birthday he invited the whole village to the restaurant.

'No one does that!' exclaimed Yves.

When everyone was seated, he walked in, arm in arm with Joelle.

'It was like his wedding night,' I suggested.

The barn and stable doors were closed. I could open the barn door because it was loosely tied with electrical wire. Inside was a nineteenth-century horse carriage. A crate with empty bottles. Some tools. Lots of hay scattered in the corners. The light was coming through the gaps in the timber panels. It had a sombre feeling of exhausted and forgotten labour.

I looked at the wall outside where we sat in the shade and played pigeon-toss with old coins. No old francs hidden in the moss. The basin where the cows drank before ambling into the barn was still dribbling with water. It was cool and delicious. On a working day we would drop bottles of cider in there to keep them cool. Today the new neighbour had deposited a slab of beer and his kid's toy boats were bobbing. I felt a bit sad. It all looked out of proportion to how I remembered it. The new entrance to Louis's house was vast. The ramp to the barn seemed too small and unstable. I decided to walk home, the long way again,

I stopped to check on the old fruit trees. I couldn't find the pear and apple trees.

The view of Mont Blanc as I walked back was stunning.

I recalled a photograph of John with Tilda Swinton walking down the same road with their hands clasped behind their backs. John is in a cream-coloured jacket and his silver hair is like the surrounding snow. Tilda is luminous and slender. To me it is also an image of the slowness of change and the austerity of the visual landscape in the village. To the left and right of John and Tilda are the signs of the church and café. These signs are still there, even though the buildings no longer function as such. The houses in the village were all built around the 1820s. The only new addition is the introduction of electricity poles, with the speed warnings and *cédez le passage* signs.

I came home, plucked a plum tomato from the kitchen bowl, and popped upstairs for a siesta.

The following day I am preparing to leave. It has an eerie feeling. No John. No Beverly. No Louis. Not even my cat Pushkin. Suddenly the house seems vast. Yves, Sandra and Vincent have driven to the Avignon Festival to see a performance of *Inventions* by the Spanish collective Mal Pelo. The performance was structured as a fugue – stretching the frontier between silence and music. It included text by John and Nick Cave. Yves was enthralled and was convinced that 'John would have loved to see his work continuing to find new life.'

The new cat in the house is Burmese. She and I are having a stand-off. She wants to come in. I am told to keep her out. The cat is begging and tapping the glass kitchen door, but I have been instructed to let her hunt for mice. She must be the only Burmese who works for a living.

In a bittersweet tone Yves said: 'You can have the feeling of us leaving you in Quincy.'

Notes

1 J. Berger, (1996) 'Will It Be a Likeness?' in *Silence Please: Stories After the Works by Juan Munoz*, ed. L. Neri, Irish Museum of Modern Art, Dublin, p. 102.

2 The exhibition curated by Merryn Gates, *What John Berger Saw*, Canberra, opened in Canberra and toured nationally between 1999–2001. There was an accompanying publication based on the symposium at Canberra which I edited, (1999), *What John Berger Saw*, ANU Canberra School of Art Publication: Canberra.

3 Jean Mohr, 2016, *John by Jean: Fifty Years of Friendship*, Cork: Occasional Press.

4 Humphrey McQueen and John Berger, (1982) 'Interviewing Berger' *Aspect: Art and Literature*, Sydney, p. 57. At the end of this interview, McQueen confesses that he has plundered some of the answers from John's prior writings, and John confides that he approved of this cubist experiment because it showed an engagement with his writing and not his personality. I had forgotten this addendum. However, the passage I quote above had been etched in my memory, and it was quite a surprise when I re-encountered it while reading the back issues of the *New Statesman* in the University Library, Cambridge – 'The Impossible Student', *The New Statesman*, 11 September 1954.

Parts of this book were previously published in *Neos Kosmos*, the anthology *A Jar of Wild Flowers: Essays in Celebration of John Berger*, and the journals *South as a State of Mind* and *Performance Paradigm*.

Works Cited

Berger, J. (1958) *A Painter of Our Time*, London: Secker & Warburg.

Berger, J. (1960) *Permanent Red*, London: Methuen.

Berger, J. (with J. Mohr) (1967) *A Fortunate Man*, Harmondsworth: Allen Lane.

Berger, J. (1972) *G: A Novel*, London: Weidenfeld & Nicholson.

Berger J. (with S. Blomberg, M. Dibb & R. Hollis) (1972) *Ways of Seeing*, Harmondsworth: Penguin.

Berger, J. (with J. Mohr & S. Blomberg) (1975) *A Seventh Man*, Harmondsworth: Penguin.

Berger, J. (1979) *Pig Earth*, London: Writers and Readers.

Berger, J. (with J. Mohr) (1982) *Another Way of Telling*, London: Writers and Readers.

Berger, J. (1982) *And Our Faces, my Heart, Brief as Photos*, London: Writers and Readers.

Berger, J. (1987) *Once in Europe*, New York: Pantheon.

Berger, J. & N. Bielski (1987) *A Question of Geography*, London: Faber & Faber.

Berger, J. (1990) *Lilac and Flag*, New York: Pantheon.

Berger, J. (1996) 'Will it be a Likeness?' in *Silence Please: Stories after the works by Juan Munoz*, ed. L. Neri, Irish Museum of Modern Art: Dublin.

Berger, J. (1995) *To the Wedding*, New York: Pantheon.

Berger, J. (1999) *King*, London: Bloomsbury.

Bourdieu, P. (2004) 'The peasant and his body', *Ethnography*, Vol 5, No 4, pp 579–599.

Buñuel, L. (1984) *My Last Breath*, London: Fontana.

Holst, G. (1975) *Road to Rembetika*, Athens: Anglo-Hellenic Publishing.

Kazantzakis, N. (1965) *Report to Greco*, London: Faber & Faber.

McQueen, H. & J. Berger, (1982) 'Interviewing Berger' *Aspect: art and literature*, Sydney.

Mohr, J. (2016), *John by Jean: Fifty Years of Friendship*, Cork: Occasional Press.

Papastergiadis, N. (1993) *Modernity as Exile: The Stranger in John Berger's Writing*, Manchester: Manchester University Press.

Papastergiadis, N. (1999), *What John Berger Saw*, ANU Canberra School of Art Publication: Canberra.

Seferis, G. (1966) *Collected Poems*, Princeton: Princeton University Press.

Sontag, S. (2001) *On Photography*, New York, Picador.

Sperling, J. (2018) *A Writer of Our Time*, London: Verso.

Serres, M. (1989) *Detachment*, Athens: Ohio University Press.

Varoufakis, Y. (2020) *Another Now*, London: Bodley Head.

Weil, S. (1951) *Waiting on God*, London: Verso.

About the Author

Nikos Papastergiadis studied at the University of Melbourne and the University of Cambridge. He was previously a lecturer and the Simon Fellow at the University of Manchester. He has published widely on contemporary art and migration. He is the director of the Research Unit in Public Cultures at the University of Melbourne, Fellow of the Australian Academy of the Humanities, and his most recent book is *The Cosmos in Cosmopolitanism* (2023).